PEGGY PORSCHEN

BOUTIQUE BAKING

delectable cakes, cupcakes and teatime treats

PHOTOGRAPHY BY
GEORGIA GLYNN SMITH

D&C
David and Charles
CINCINNATI, OHIO

For my darling husband Bryn,
for letting me have my "pink" cake store
and for giving it your all and more.

Editorial director Jane O'Shea
Creative director Helen Lewis
Project editor Lisa Pendreigh
Assistant Editor Louise McKeever
Designer Helen Bratby
Photographer Georgia Glynn Smith
Stylist Vicky Sullivan
Production director Vincent Smith
Production controller Aysun Hughes

www.fwmedia.com
16 15 14 13 12 5 4 3 2 1

Distributed in Canada by Fraser Direct
100 Armstrong Avenue
Georgetown, ON, Canada L7G 5S4
Tel: (905) 877-4411

SRN: V9296
ISBN-13: 978-1-4402-2368-6
ISBN-10: 1-4402-2306-8

CONTENTS

WELCOME TO BOUTIQUE BAKING

It is a pleasure to introduce my new book, which is based on delicious recipes from my latest venture, the Peggy Porschen Parlour. After seven successful years of running a bespoke cake design company I have finally fulfilled my lifelong dream of opening my first cake boutique, based in London's beautiful Belgravia. Filled with delicious cakes and confections, complementing blends of artisan teas and coffees, the parlour has often been described as "cake heaven."

I have always had a passion for baking exquisite cakes. My earliest childhood memories go back to my very first birthday, sitting next to a beautiful marzipan-covered birthday cake with "Peggy 1" frosted on top. Over the following years, eating birthday cake and baking Christmas cookies with my mom and brother were the annual highlights. I started making my own cakes from the age of 14 and soon I knew that there was nothing I would rather do, so I decided to pursue a career in cakes. Coming from a nation famed for its baking and cake culture, the taste has always been as important to me as the look of a cake so I enrolled at London's school for culinary arts, Le Cordon Bleu, where I completed the Grand Diplôme de Cuisine et Pâtisserie. I later worked for some of the most renowned pastry kitchens in the UK before launching my own business, Peggy Porschen Cakes, in 2003. The business immediately took off and soon I was making cakes for well-known celebrities, quickly establishing myself as one of London's leading names in cake design. In 2005, I published my first book **Pretty Party Cakes** which won the Gourmand World Cook Book Award for "Best Entertaining Cook Book." The company has since gone from strength to strength and if you asked me how many cakes I have made since the beginning, I could not possibly tell you.

Opened in October 2010, the Peggy Porschen Parlour has given me the opportunity to create my first "ready-to-eat" collection of cupcakes, layer cakes, and seasonal bakes. Where previously I created exclusive made-to-order cakes for events, my cakes are now accessible to a wider audience. Those of you

who are familiar with my work are aware of just how much I care about making baked goods look perfectly beautiful. When the opportunity of opening the Parlour came along, I was faced with a tough challenge —to create a collection of everyday cakes and bakes that taste utterly delicious and, at the same time, stand proudly next to exquisite celebration cakes. It took months of test baking, tasting, trial, and error, but the hard work was worthwhile. In Summer 2011, less than one year after opening, we were awarded five gold stars by the Guild of Fine Foods Great Taste Awards. The menu at the Parlour is a favorite among our local Belgravia customers, and I take great joy and satisfaction in developing seasonal treats and ideas.

I decided to share a selection of my favorites with you in **Boutique Baking**, the first book inspired by my work at the parlor. Filled with a mouthwatering array of cakes, home-bakes, and confections, many ideas are inspired by old-time favorites, such as the Chocolate Battenberg and Morello Cherry Bakewell Tarts, seasonal influences for Christmas and Spring, and

recipes inspired by my German roots such as gorgeous Springerle Cookies and sumptuous Black Forest Cupcakes. I have also added a selection of drinks recipes to complement my confections and inspire perfect tea party menus.

I have taken great care to ensure each recipe is suitable for bakers of all experience levels and have set out to demonstrate that, by using simple tools and easy techniques, one can take a plain cake or cookie and without fuss or expertize give it an utterly charming and professional finish. For the more experienced bakers who cherish a decorative challenge, I have slipped in a few slightly more intricate designs, such as my Gingerbread Village, a beautiful Raspberry & Rose Dome Cake as well as a stunning Christmas cake idea.

Writing this book has helped me to rediscover just how much I love to bake. I find it fun and therapeutic and I truly believe that cakes can make people happy. I hope that you will feel enticed and enjoy baking recipes from this book, and that it will become an invaluable source of inspiration for many years to come. Enjoy!

Peggy

SWEET TREATS

MERINGUE KISSES

PRETTY PASTEL-COLORED MINI MERINGUES ARE SIMPLE AND YET SO ADORABLE;
THEY ADD A LOVELY TOUCH TO A TABLE FOR ANY OCCASION. DISPLAYED
IN CHIC CANDY JARS, THEY LOOK DELICIOUS. WITH A VERY LONG SHELF LIFE,
THEY ARE THE PERFECT GIFT WHEN WRAPPED IN CELLOPHANE BAGS.

Makes approximately 100 meringues

ingredients

3½ ounces egg whites (3 large eggs)
Pinch of salt
½ cup superfine sugar
1 teaspoon vanilla extract
Scant 1 cup confectioners' sugar, sifted
Pink, blue, and yellow liquid food color

equipment

Basic baking kit (see page 172)
3 large plastic pastry bags
3 star piping tips

Preheat the oven to 176 degrees F. Line two cookie sheets with waxed paper.

Place the egg whites and a pinch of salt into the bowl of an electric mixer and start whisking at high speed. Make sure that the bowl is entirely grease-free before you start, otherwise the egg whites will not whip up properly.

As the egg whites are stiffening, slowly sprinkle the superfine sugar into the mix. Stop whisking as the meringue becomes stiffer and glossy; be careful not to overwhisk the mixture.

Add the vanilla extract and slowly fold the confectioners' sugar into the meringue mixture using a rubber spatula.

Separate the meringue mix into three equal parts; keep the first white, mix the second with pink liquid food color to a pastel pink shade, and the third with blue and yellow liquid food color for a pastel aqua shade.

Place a star tip in each of the pastry bags then fill each one with a different colored meringue mixture. Pipe little rosettes onto the cookie sheets lined with waxed paper.

Place the meringues in the preheated oven for between 2 to 3 hours or until they have fully dried out.

Stored in a dry, airtight container, these mini meringue kisses can last for up to 3 months.

CHOCOLATE CRUNCH CAKE
WITH MARSHMALLOWS AND PISTACHIOS

THIS RECIPE WAS INTRODUCED TO THE PARLOUR IN CELEBRATION OF THE ROYAL WEDDING OF WILLIAM AND CATHERINE, AFTER I LEARNED THAT CHOCOLATE FRIDGE CAKE IS WILLIAM'S FAVORITE DESSERT AND WAS TO BE SERVED AT THE WEDDING BREAKFAST. IT HAS BEEN SO POPULAR AMONG OUR CUSTOMERS THAT THIS CHOCOLATE CAKE HAS EARNED A SPOT IN THIS BOOK.

Makes one 8"-square cake

ingredients

Scant 1 cup unsalted butter, softened
1 pound 5 ouces semisweet chocolate (minimum 53% cocoa solids), chopped or in buttons
6 tablespoons dark corn syrup
10½ ounces Rich Tea cookies, roughly broken
½ cup peeled pistachios, roughly chopped
½ cup peeled hazelnuts, roasted and crushed
3 ounces small pink and white marshmallows

equipment

Basic baking kit (see page 172)
8"-square cake pan or deep cookie sheet of a similar size

Line the cake pan or cookie sheet with waxed paper.

Place the butter, chocolate, and dark corn syrup in a large plastic bowl and gently melt in the microwave at medium heat. Alternatively, place the ingredients in a pan and gently melt, stirring occasionally, until smooth.

In a separate bowl, mix the broken cookies with the chopped and crushed nuts and the marshmallows. Add to the chocolate mixture and stir until well combined.

Pour the cake mixture into the prepared pan or sheet, then spread it evenly using a rubber spatula. Chill in the refrigerator until firm and set. Cut into bars of approximately 1" thick.

Stored in the refrigerator, the chocolate crunch cake can last for up to 1 week.

MORELLO CHERRY BAKEWELL TARTS

A MODERN TAKE ON A BRITISH TEATIME FAVORITE: THE CLASSIC BAKEWELL TART.
TO KEEP WITH THE CHERRY THEME, SIMPLY DECORATE THE TARTS
WITH SUGAR CHERRIES AND PINK FONDANT.

Makes approximately 20 tarts

ingredients

For the sweet pie dough
11 tablespoons unsalted butter, softened
½ cup superfine sugar
1 ounce egg (½ large egg), beaten
Scant 1½ cups all-purpose flour
½ cup ground almonds
Pinch of salt

For the frangipan
½ cup unsalted butter, softened
Generous ½ cup superfine sugar
Finely grated zest of 1 lemon
1 teaspoon almond extract
1 medium egg
1¼ cups ground almonds
Generous ¼ cup self-rising flour
Pinch of salt

For the filling
scant ½ cup good-quality Morello
cherry jam

For the decoration
2 tablespoons apricot jam, strained
1 pound 2 ounces liquid fondant
1 teaspoon glucose
A small amount of simple sugar syrup
(if required, see pages 61–2)
A small amount of rolled fondant
A small amount of royal icing
(see pages 182–3)
Pink, red, green, and brown
food color

equipment

Basic baking kit (see page 172)
20 fluted mini tart pans
Spray oil
Plastic pastry bag
Small leaf cutter
Paper pastry bags (see page 184)
Sugar thermometer

Preheat the oven to 320 degrees F.

To make the sweet pie dough

Place the butter and superfine sugar in a mixing bowl and cream together until just combined: do not to make it too fluffy. Gradually add the beaten egg to the mixture.

Sift the flour, almonds, and salt into a separate bowl. Add in batches to the butter mixture until just combined. Wrap the dough in plastic wrap and chill for at least 1 hour.

To make the frangipan

Beat the butter, sugar, lemon zest, and almond extract until pale and fluffy. Continue whisking and slowly add the egg.

Sift the almonds, flour, and salt into a separate bowl. Add in batches to the butter mix until just combined.

To assemble the tarts

Roll out the dough to a thickness of ⅙ to ⅛". Place it into lightly greased tart pans. Fill the bottoms of the shells with 1 teaspoon of cherry jam. Chill for 30 minutes.

Place the frangipan into a pastry bag and fill the tart shells to just below the top edge. Make sure you leave a little room at the top as the frangipan will expand during baking.

Bake in a preheated oven for about 15 to 20 minutes, until the tops are brown and the frangipan is cooked through. Remove the tarts from the pans while still warm and let cool.

To decorate

Once cool, heat the apricot jam until it is smooth and runny. Brush the jam thinly over the tops of the tarts and let set.

Heat the fondant in a small pan over medium heat, but be careful not to let it boil. It should have a dipping temperature of approximately 118 to 126 degrees F and a thick but runny pouring consistency. Should the consistency be too thick at the correct temperature, dilute it with a little sugar syrup.

Add the glucose and the pink food color to make a soft pink shade. Place the fondant into a deep bowl that will allow for dipping.

Pick one tart up at a time and hold it upside down, dipping it into the hot fondant up to the fluted edge of the tart shell. Lift out and spin it fast to let the excess fondant drip off and let set.

If the first dip is not perfect, double dip it once the first layer has set. Make sure that your fondant is always hot and runny when dipping and reheat from time to time as required.

Mix two-thirds of the rolled fondant with the red food coloring to create a cherry red shade. Shape into small equal-size balls with your hands, making 2 balls per tart.

Mix the last third of rolled fondant with green food coloring and using a small rolling pin, roll the fondant out on a surface dusted with confectioners' sugar until ⅟₃₂ to ⅟₁₆" thick. Cut out small leaf shapes and score the center with the back of a small kitchen knife.

Mix a small amount of the royal icing with brown food color to a soft-peak consistency (see page 183). Fill a paper pastry bag with the brown icing. Snip a small tip off the end of the bag and pipe the cherry stems onto the tarts. Stick the cherries and leaves on top using the remaining brown icing.

ICE-CREAM CAKE POPS

I SIMPLY COULDN'T IGNORE THE CURRENT CRAZE FOR CAKE POPS
AND HERE I HAVE COME UP WITH MY OWN VERSION USING DIPPING FONDANT
OR FONDANT PATISSIERE. THE TEXTURE IS SMOOTH AND SHINY,
AND INSTANTLY MELTS IN YOUR MOUTH.

Makes approximately 12 cake pops

ingredients

14 ounces vanilla sponge (½ recipe quantity,
see page 116)
1 pound 5 ounces soft ganache (see page 105)
12 small ice-cream wafer cones
Approximately 5 cups superfine sugar or
enough to fill a small bowl
1 pound 5 ounces liquid fondant (also called
fondant patissiere)
1 teaspoon glucose
A small amount of simple sugar syrup
(if required, see pages 61–2)
A selection of food colors
Sugar sprinkles

equipment

Basic baking kit (see page 172)
Tray
Rubber gloves (optional)
Plastic pastry bag
12 plastic drinking cups
Sugar thermometer

Following the recipe on page 116, make a vanilla sponge. Following the recipe on page 105, make a ganache. Let cool until it has a soft buttery texture.

Fill a few small plastic bowls with 2 pounds 4 ounces superfine sugar and compress as much as possible. This will provide a stand for the ice-cream cones while the fondant icing sets.

Line a tray with waxed paper.

To make the cake balls
Break the sponge cake down into crumbs and place in a mixing bowl. Add the ganache a little at a time and combine until all the cake crumbs stick together. Using your hands, shape into 12 equal-size balls and place them on the prepared tray. You may want to use rubber gloves when doing this as it is a very messy job. Chill in the freezer until firmly set.

To assemble the cake pops
Place the remaining ganache into a plastic pastry bag. Cut 1″ from the tip of the bag. Pipe the ganache into a wafer cone until it just reaches the top. Place one chilled cake ball on top and press down to ensure it sticks to the ganache. Stand the cone in a plastic cup and place it back in the freezer to set. Repeat for all the remaining cones and cake balls.

TO ASSEMBLE THE CAKE POPS, FILL THE WAFER CONES WITH GANACHE AND PRESS A CHILLED CAKE BALL ON TOP. ONCE IT HAS SET, DIP THE CAKE BALL INTO LIQUID FONDANT AND TOP WITH MULTICOLORED SUGAR SPRINKLES.

To decorate

Melt the fondant in the microwave on medium heat until runny. Make sure that it does not boil as it will lose its shine. Stir in the glucose and add some sugar syrup to adjust the consistency if required. You want it to be a thick pouring consistency with a dipping temperature of about 118 to 126 degrees F. This temperature will ensure that the fondant sets immediately after dipping.

Divide the fondant into equal parts and mix with your chosen food colors. Use small bowls with enough depth for dipping the balls.

Take one cake pop at a time and dip it upside down into the fondant right up until it reaches the edge of the wafer cone. Lift out and spin the remaining fondant off. Top with sugar sprinkles while the fondant is still soft.

Push the cone into the bowl filled with superfine sugar and let it set. You can place a few cones next to each other but make sure they do not touch.

These cake pops will last for up to 5 days when kept at room temperature. Do not refrigerate as the fondant will melt.

PEGGY'S SIGNATURE MACARONS

THIS RECIPE IS FOR THE MORE EXPERIENCED BAKER AS IT REQUIRES
PATIENCE AND PRECISION. BUT DON'T FEEL PUT OFF, ONCE MASTERED IT IS
SO WORTHWHILE. I USE MY OWN PURPLE RASPBERRY AND ROSE JAM
FOR THE FILLING, BUT YOU CAN CREATE YOUR OWN FLAVOR COMBINATIONS.

Makes approximately 50 macarons or 100 shells

ingredients

2¼ cups ground almonds
1¾ cups confectioner's sugar
7 ounces egg whites
1 cup superfine sugar
Scant ½ cup water
Food color (optional)

equipment

Basic baking kit (see page 172)
Permanent marker pen
Round piping tip, ½" in diameter
(I use a No. 12 from Wiltons)
Small heart-shape cookie cutter (optional)
Sugar thermometer
Plastic pastry bags

Preheat the oven to 300 degrees F. Prepare the oven trays for the macarons. Cut sheets of baking parchment to fit a couple of oven trays. Using the fat end of a large round piping tip and a small heart-shape cookie cutter as templates, draw circles and hearts on the reverse side of the parchment at even intervals.

In a food processor, briefly pulse together the ground almonds and confectioners' sugar until mixed well and sift into a large bowl. Set aside (this is known as a "tant pour tant").

To make an Italian meringue, place the egg white in a clean, dry bowl. Reserve 1 tablespoon of the egg white to mix with the coloring later on.

Place the superfine sugar in a small pan with the water. Dissolve the sugar over medium heat, then bring the sugar syrup to a boil. Using a sugar thermometer, measure the temperature of the syrup. When the syrup reaches 239 degrees F, start to slowly whisk the egg whites. Gradually increasing the whisking speed until the eggs are white and frothy. Once the syrup reaches 250 degrees F, slow down the whisking and carefully pour the hot syrup into the egg whites in a thin steady stream—pour down the side of the bowl so that the syrup does not splash onto the whisk.

Once all the syrup has been incorporated, continue whisking quickly until the meringue has cooled to room temperature; this will take about 5 to 10 minutes.

Once the meringue has cooled, add your preferred coloring to the reserved tablespoon of egg white and then whisk into the meringue.

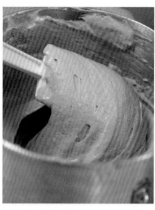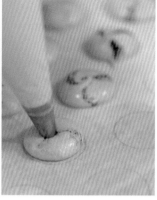

FOR A CANDY STRIPE SWIRL, PAINT THREE STRIPES OF FOOD COLOR DOWN THE INSIDE OF THE TIP BEFORE FITTING IT IN THE BAG, FILLING WITH MIXTURE AND PIPING.

Using the rubber spatula, fold the "tant pour tant" into the meringue in three batches. Fold gently but thoroughly to ensure the mix is loose and smooth when piped. The amount you fold in here and the consistency you achieve is crucial; you want the mix to be even and fall easily off the spatula, but not so liquid that it does not keep a good round shape when piped.

Place the tip into the pastry bag. Using a rubber spatula, half fill the pastry bag with macaron mixture.

Use a little of the macaron mix to secure the sheets of baking parchment in place; smear a small amount of mixture on each corner of the underside of the sheet.

Using the circles you have drawn as a guide, pipe the small circles. To finish piping the circle, stop applying pressure to the bag and flick the tip around in a small circular motion as you pull away. This ensures there will be no peak on top of the macaron.

For the hearts, pipe a blob at the top half of the heart and then drag it down to the bottom. Repeat on the other side. If the mixture is the correct consistency, any small trails should sink back to leave a smooth surface.

Once the macarons are all piped, gently tap the tray on the work surface to bring any large air bubbles to the surface and pop them with a toothpick. Let the macarons dry out a little on the surface; 15 to 30 minutes in dry conditions. You should be able to touch the surface of the macaron without your finger sticking.

As soon as the macarons have a dry skin, place them on the lower shelves in the oven and immediately reduce the heat to 275 degrees F. If your oven bakes from the top, then place a tray on the shelf above the macarons to prevent the tops from browning too much.

Bake for approximately 15 minutes, turning the trays halfway through the cooking time. The macarons are done when the tops are dry. As soon as they are done, remove the tray from the oven and transfer the baking parchment, with the macarons still attached, directly onto a wet dishtowel. Leave for a few minutes and then remove the macarons.

Store in an airtight container at room temperature for up to two days or in the freezer for longer. Sandwich with your chosen filling on the day of consumption, and once filled refrigerate for one hour before eating —this helps the macarons to soften and the flavors to develop.

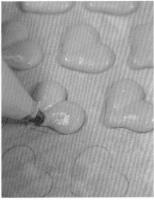

TO MAKE A HEART, PIPE A BLOB AT THE TOP AND DRAG IT
DOWNWARD. REPEAT ON THE OTHER SIDE.

flavors

Raspberry and Rose Color the macaron mixture with pink food color. When piping, paint the inside of the tip with three thick lines of claret paste food color to achieve the "candy stripe" look. Sandwich the shells together with raspberry and rose jam—thicken the jam slightly by heating it for 3 to 4 minutes in a microwave. Cool slightly before spreading.

Chocolate Replace ½ cup of the almonds with ½ cup unsweetened cocoa powder, then proceed as normal with the recipe. If desired, add a little brown food color to the macaron mixture to achieve a darker color. Sandwich the shells together with dark chocolate ganache (see page 105).

troubleshooting

Egg whites These should be separated a few days in advance and left uncovered in the refrigerator to allow some of the moisture to evaporate and strengthen the whites. Bring the egg whites to room temperature before using. If in doubt, add a teaspoon of Meri-White to the egg whites to counteract any "watery-ness."

Macaronage This is the stage of folding the "tant pour tant" into the meringue. The consistency achieved is very important—if the mixture is too stiff then the tops will not be smooth after piping; if the mixture is too liquid then it will not keep a good shape and may produce grease spots on the surface of the macaron after baking. If in doubt, test a little of the mix by dropping a teaspoonful onto the oven tray and pulling a little peak up on the surface. If it is ready, the top should sink back into the surface gradually. If the peak stays there, the mix needs to be folded a little longer. Drying It is important to let your macarons dry on the surface before baking. If you do not let them dry, the tops will not be smooth and produce a good "foot" on the bottom. If you dry them for too long, they will be smooth but not produce a foot at all.

Baking Every oven is different, so it is important to get to know your own oven and what temperature works best. Generally, a low temperature is important to prevent overbrowning of the macarons and a low shelf for the same reason. Some chefs find the macarons can bake too quickly on the bottom and therefore recommend using two trays, one on top of the other, to bake your macarons—I find they can brown on top more easily so tend to place a tray on the rack above instead. If you bake the macarons for too long, they will lift easily off the paper but be a bit dry and possibly overbrown; to counteract the dryness you can place them in an airtight container in the refrigerator for a day to soften. If they are not baked enough, they will be too soft and not lift off the parchment properly; they will also sink back down and develop what look like grease spots on the top.

MINI CINNAMON DOUGHNUTS

THESE ARE LOVELY LITTLE TREATS THAT NOT ONLY LOOK PRETTY AND TASTE YUMMY
BUT THEY ARE ALSO LOW IN FAT AS THEY ARE BAKED RATHER THAN FRIED.
WHEN PACKAGED IN NICE PRESENTATION BOXES THEY MAKE CUTE GIFTS.

Makes approximately 36 doughnuts

ingredients

Generous ¾ cup all-purpose flour
½ teaspoon baking powder
¼ teaspoon ground cinnamon
Pinch of salt
⅓ cup superfine sugar
⅛ cup light brown sugar
1 medium egg
Scant ¼ cup whole milk
Scant ¼ cup buttermilk
½ teaspoon vanilla extract
1 tablespoon unsalted butter, melted
1 pound 5 ounces liquid fondant (also called
fondant patissiere)
1 teaspoon glucose
A small amount of simple sugar syrup
(if required, see pages 61–2)
A selection of liquid food colors
1¾ ounces semisweet chocolate, melted

equipment

Basic baking kit (see page 172)
3 mini doughnut oven trays
Spray oil
Plastic pastry bag (optional)
Sugar thermometer

Preheat the oven to 325 degrees F. Prepare the mini doughnut oven trays by greasing each mold with spray oil.

Sift together the flour, baking powder, ground cinnamon, salt, and sugars into a mixing bowl. In a separate bowl whisk together the egg, milk, buttermilk, vanilla extract, and melted butter.

Pour the liquid ingredients onto the dry ingredients, mixing briefly until just combined.

Pipe or pour the mix into the prepared trays, filling only just halfway.

Bake for 10 to 12 minutes until the tops spring back to the touch and have lightly browned.

Melt the fondant in the microwave on medium heat until runny. Make sure that it does not boil as the fondant will lose its shine. Stir in the glucose and add some sugar syrup to adjust the consistency, if required. You want it to be a thick pouring consistency. The temperature of the fondant must be about 118 to 126 degrees F: this ensures that the fondant sets immediately after dipping.

Divide the liquid fondant equally between small, deep bowls and mix with your chosen food colors.

Dip each doughnut upside down into the fondant until half coated. Let set slightly then drizzle with the melted chocolate using a teaspoon or fork. Let set.

MARSHMALLOW PUFFS

SERVE THESE CHEERING MARSHMALLOW PUFFS WITH A CUP OF HOMEMADE HOT CHOCOLATE (SEE PAGES 164-5). I MADE MINE INTO DOME SHAPES BUT YOU CAN ALSO SPREAD THE MARSHMALLOW ON A TRAY THEN USE COOKIE CUTTERS TO MAKE FUN SHAPES.

Makes approximately 60 to 70 small puffs

ingredients

1¼ cups water
6 sheets gelatin
Generous 3 cups superfine sugar
4½ ounces glucose
2½ ounces egg whites (approximately 2 large eggs), at room temperature
Pinch of salt
Seeds of 1 vanilla bean
Pink, purple, and green liquid food color

equipment

Basic baking kit (see page 172)
Sugar thermometer
Plastic pastry bags
Silicone trays with dome shape wells of approximately 1¾" diameter
Spray oil

Place the gelatin in a pan with generous ½ cup of the water. Let soak for 10 to 15 minutes. Gently warm the gelatin until the leaves have dissolved. Alternatively, dissolve the gelatin by microwaving it in short bursts on low-medium heat.

Place scant 1⅔ cups of the superfine sugar and the glucose in a small pan with the remaining water. Gently warm over low heat until the sugar has dissolved, then turn up the heat and bring the syrup to a boil.

Using a sugar thermometer, measure the temperature of the syrup. When the syrup reaches 239 degrees F, place the egg whites in a mixing bowl with the dissolved gelatin and salt and start whisking. Once the syrup reaches 250 degrees F, slow down the whisking and carefully pour the syrup into the egg whites in a thin steady stream—pour down the side of the bowl so that the syrup does not splash onto the whisk.

Once all the syrup has been incorporated into the egg whites, continue whisking quickly until the marshmallow has cooled to room temperature. Once the marshmallow has cooled, add the vanilla seeds.

For a combination of colors, divide the mix into equal parts and fold the liquid food color through with a spatula. Place each colored mixture into a separate pastry bag using a rubber spatula. Cut approximately 1" from the tip of the bag and pipe the marshmallow into the greased molds. Let dry for several hours.

In the meantime, make the colored sprinkling sugars. Divide the remaining superfine sugar evenly between 3 bowls and mix each with a few drops of liquid food color, matching the colors of the marshmallows. Sift out any lumps before use.

Once the marshmallows are fully set, remove them from the molds and roll in their coordinating sprinkling sugars. Let the marshmallows dry uncovered overnight before packing into airtight containers. The marshmallows can be stored like this for up to 5 days.

BEAUTIFUL
COOKIES

CITRUS BUTTERFLY COOKIES

BEAUTIFUL BUTTERFLIES WITH A FRESH AND ZESTY ZING MAKE THE PERFECT
ACCOMPANIMENT FOR AN AROMATIC CUP OF TEA. THE CLEVER YET
MINIMAL DECORATION LENDS AN INTRICATE HANDMADE FEEL ADDING
A TOUCH OF FINESSE WITHOUT COMPROMISING TASTE.

Makes approximately 25 cookies

ingredients

1⅛ cups unsalted butter, softened
1¼ cups superfine sugar
Pinch of salt
For orange cookies
Finely grated zest of 2 oranges
For lemon cookies
Finely grated zest of 3 lemons
For lime cookies
Finely grated zest of 3 limes
1 large egg
3½ cups all-purpose flour, plus extra for
dusting
Confectioners' sugar, for dusting

equipment

Basic baking kit (see page 172)
Selection of butterfly cookie cutters
Selection of laser-cut cake or cookie stencils,
or alternatively use doilies

Preheat the oven to 315 degrees F. Line a cookie sheet with waxed paper.

To make the cookies
Place the butter, sugar, salt, and preferred zest in a mixing bowl and cream together until smooth and creamy in texture.

Beat the egg lightly in another bowl and slowly add to the butter mixture while whisking until well incorporated.

Sift in the flour and mix until the dough just comes together. Gather the dough into a ball, wrap in plastic wrap, and chill for at least 30 minutes or until the dough feels firm and cool.

Place the dough on a floured surface and knead briefly.

Roll out the dough to a thickness of approximately ⅛ to ⅙". Using a selection of butterfly cookie cutters, cut out the butterfly shapes and place them onto the prepared cookie sheet. Chill again for 30 minutes or until cool and firm.

Bake for 6 minutes or until the cookies are golden brown around the edges.

Once the cookies are baked, let them rest for about 30 minutes outside of the oven.

To decorate
Once cool, place either the stencils or the doilies on top of the cookies. Using a fine strainer, lightly dust the cookies with confectioners' sugar. Carefully lift the stencils off to reveal pretty patterns.

tip

Always bake cookies of the same size together on a sheet,
otherwise the smaller ones will burn while the larger ones are baking.

SPRINGERLE COOKIES

SPRINGERLE ORIGINATE FROM GERMANY AND ARE TRADITIONALLY MADE USING
HAND-CARVED WOODEN MOLDS. THE RECIPE CONTAINS HARTSHORN SALT
AS A RAISING AGENT, WHICH ALLOWS THEM TO KEEP THEIR SHAPE.
MADE AROUND CHRISTMAS TIME, THEY ARE PERFECT AS TREE DECORATIONS AND GIFTS.

Makes approximately 20 cookies

ingredients

¼ teaspoon Hartshorn salt (baker's
ammonia), alternatively use baking powder
1 tablespoon milk
3 medium eggs
Scant 3⅓ cups confectioners' sugar
Finely grated zest of 1 lemon
3½ tablespoons salted butter, softened
3½ cups all-purpose flour, plus extra for
dusting

equipment

Basic baking kit (see page 172)
Selection of wooden Springerle molds

Make the dough one or two days before baking.

To make the cookies
Place the Hartshorn salt and milk together in a small bowl. Mix and set aside. Please note that the Hartshorn salt will give off a strong smell.

In a separate bowl, whisk the eggs until they are thick and frothy and have a slight yellow color. Gradually add the confectioners' sugar, lemon zest, and butter in small chunks, then add the Hartshorn mixture. Mix for another 30 minutes.

Gradually add the flour. Once the dough becomes too difficult to mix, knead in any remaining flour, a little at a time. The texture should be light and not too sticky. Once the dough reaches the required consistency, don't add any more flour as the dough will harden too fast.

On a floured surface roll out the dough to a thickness of ½ to ⅝". Press the mold firmly into the dough and lift off. Using a knife, trim any excess dough from the edges of the embossed design. Alternatively, use a cookie cutter if you have one the correct size. For circles or ovals, trim around the mold on the dough before lifting off to ensure the shape does not tear.

Transfer the cookies onto a cookie sheet lined with waxed paper. Let them air dry for 24 to 48 hours, depending on size.

Preheat the oven to 437 degrees F and bake for 15 to 20 minutes, depending on size, or until the cookies are light golden brown on the bottom but remain white on top. During baking the bases puff up leaving the tops in perfect shape.

These cookies are soft and chewy in texture, however they harden quite quickly. Stored in an airtight container they keep for up to one month or, if for decorative purposes only, they last for several months.

BLOSSOM COOKIES

THIS IS A VERY QUICK AND EASY WAY TO DECORATE AN OTHERWISE PLAIN COOKIE, USING A SIMPLE SILICONE MOLD TO MAKE ROLLED FONDANT BLOSSOMS. MADE IN A SELECTION OF PRETTY COLORS, THESE COOKIES MAKE FABULOUS PRESENTS OR PARTY FAVORS.

Makes approximately 30 to 40 cookies

ingredients

Scant 1 cup unsalted butter, softened
1 cup superfine sugar
Seeds of 1 vanilla bean
Pinch of salt
1 medium egg
Scant 3½ cups all-pupose flour, plus extra for dusting
1 pound 5 ounces rolled fondant
2 teaspoons gum tragacanth
Yellow, orange, pink, and red paste food color
A small amount of white vegetable fat (optional)
A small amount of apricot jam, strained

equipment

Basic baking kit (see page 172)
1½–2"-round cookie cutter
Chrysanthemum silicone mold
(I use a mold from
First Impressions)

Preheat the oven to 347 degrees F. Line two cookie sheets with waxed paper.

To make the cookies
Place the butter, sugar, vanilla seeds, and salt in a mixing bowl and cream together until smooth and creamy in texture.

Beat the egg lightly in another bowl and slowly add to the butter mixture while whisking until well incorporated.

Sift in the flour and mix until the dough just comes together. Gather the dough into a ball, wrap in plastic wrap, and chill for at least 30 minutes or until the dough feels firm and cool.

Place the dough on a floured surface and knead briefly. Roll out the dough to a thickness of ⅛ to ¼". Using a round cookie cutter, cut out 30 circles and place them onto the prepared cookie sheets. Chill again for 30 minutes or until cool and firm.

Bake for 6 minutes or until the cookies are golden brown around the edges. Once the cookies are baked, let them rest for about 30 minutes outside of the oven.

To decorate
Knead the rolled fondant with the gum tragacanth until it starts feeling firm and stretchy.

Divide the rolled fondant into four equal parts. Mix the first with a small amount of yellow paste food color to a pale lemon shade, the second with orange to a pale peach shade, and the third with pink to a pale pink shade. To create a coral shade, combine a little of the red and orange paste food colors and use to color the fourth part. If the rolled fondant sticks to your fingers while coloring, add a small amout of vegetable fat.

Once the rolled fondant is colored, cover with plastic wrap to prevent it from drying out. Let rest for 30 minutes to firm up a little.

Following the instructions on page 175, make a chrysanthemum blossom for each cookie using the different color rolled fondants.

To stick the blossoms to the tops of the cookies, gently heat the apricot jam in a pan. Brush a thin layer of the jam over each cookie then place the blossoms on top. Let set.

TEASPOON CHOCOLATE COOKIES

IT'S ALL IN THE LITTLE DETAILS ... A DAINTY CHOCOLATE COOKIE SPOON
CAN ADD THAT SPECIAL TOUCH TO A SIMPLE CUP OF TEA.

Makes approximately 30 cookies

ingredients

Scant 1 cup unsalted butter, softened
1 cup superfine sugar
Pinch of salt
1 medium egg
2½ cups all-purpose flour, sifted, plus extra
for dusting
½ cup unsweetened cocoa powder, sifted

equipment

Basic baking kit (see page 172)
Teaspoon cookie cutter (I use one from a
teatime cookie cutter set)

Preheat the oven to 147 degrees F. Line a cookie sheet with waxed paper.

To make the cookies
Place the butter, sugar, and salt in a mixing bowl and cream together until smooth and creamy in texture.

Beat the egg lightly in another bowl and slowly add to the butter mixture while whisking until well incorporated.

Sift in the flour and cocoa powder and mix until the dough just comes together. Gather the dough into a ball, wrap in plastic wrap, and chill for at least 30 minutes or until the dough feels firm and cool.

Place the dough on a floured surface and knead briefly. Roll out the dough to a thickness of approximately ⅛ to ⅙". Using a teaspoon cookie cutter, cut out the spoon shapes and place them onto the prepared cookie sheet. Chill again for 30 minutes or until cool and firm.

Bake for 6 minutes or until the cookies spring back to the touch. Once the cookies are baked, let them rest for about 30 minutes outside of the oven.

YOU NEED TWO PAPER PASTRY BAGS FOR EACH COLOR: ONE FILLED WITH SOFT-PEAK ICING
FOR THE OUTLINES AND ANOTHER FILLED WITH RUNNY ICING TO FLOOD THE SHAPES.

COOKIE ADVENT CALENDAR

THIS IS A LOVELY IDEA FOR A HOMEMADE ADVENT CALENDAR.
TO HANG ON A WALL, STICK THE COOKIES TO A CAKE BOARD
THAT HAS BEEN COVERED WITH ROLLED FONDANT.
ALTERNATIVELY, HANG THE COOKIES WITH RIBBON
ON A CHRISTMAS TREE OR WREATH.

Makes approximately 24 cookies

ingredients

1 recipe quantity of gingerbread dough
(see page 48)
All-purpose flour, for dusting
1 pound 5 ounces royal icing
(see pages 182–3)
Red, green, pink, ivory, black, and orange
paste food color
Edible gold luster
Small amount of clear alcohol, such as vodka
Small amount of piping gel

equipment

Basic baking kit (see page 172)
Selection of Christmas-themed cookie
cutters (such as Santa Claus, snowman,
snowflake, Christmas tree, sleigh,
bauble, star, candy cane, holly leaf,
stocking) and one square cookie cutter
Paper pastry bags (see page 184)
Resealable plastic bags
Flat, wide paintbrush

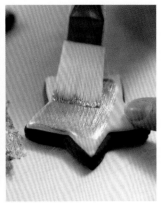

WHEN USING EDIBLE LUSTER, FIRST ICE THE COOKIE WITH IVORY-COLORED ICING AS THIS PROVIDES A GOOD BASE FOR THE GOLD POWDER.

Preheat the oven to 350 degrees F. Line two cookie sheets with waxed paper.

To make the cookies
On a floured surface roll out the gingerbread dough to a thickness of approximately 1/6 to ¼". Using your selection of Christmas-themed cookie cutters, cut out the various shapes and place them onto the prepared cookie sheets. Chill for at least 30 minutes.

Bake for 6 to 8 minutes, depending on size, or until the cookies spring back to the touch and are slightly darker around the edges.

Once the cookies are baked, let them rest for about 30 minutes outside of the oven.

To ice the cookies
Following the instructions on page 184, prepare the paper pastry bags. You need two pastry bags for each color of icing: one filled with soft-peak icing to pipe the outlines and one filled with runny icing to flood the outlined shapes. Once prepared, keep each pastry bag in a resealable plastic bag to prevent the icing from drying out between use.

When icing cookies, always outline and flood one color at a time, allowing the icing to dry completely before adding the next color to the cookie. This helps to prevent the different colors from bleeding into each other.

For each color, take the pastry bag filled with soft-peak icing and cut a small section from the tip of the pastry bag. Trace the outline of the colored area onto the cookie. Then take the pastry bag filled with runny icing in the corresponding color and use this to flood the center of the outlined area.

Once all the cookies have been flooded and allowed to dry completely, use the soft-peak icing in various colors to pipe on any additional detail required.

The snowflake cookies are not flooded with icing, instead the detail is piped directly onto the cookies using white soft-peak icing.

To decorate with gold luster
Ice the cookies with ivory colored icing and let dry. This provides a good base for gold luster. Mix small amounts of luster powder, clear alcohol, and piping gel to create a thick paste. Using a flat, wide paintbrush, brush the paste all over the ivory icing and let dry.

GINGERBREAD VILLAGE

CREATE A CHARMING COLLECTION OF GINGERBREAD HOUSES,
PEOPLE, AND SNOWFLAKES TO HANG ON THE CHRISTMAS TREE:
A BEAUTIFUL WINTER-WONDERLAND DISPLAY.

Makes approximately 25 to 30 cookies, depending on size

ingredients

5 tablespoons water
Generous 1 cup light brown sugar
3 tablespoons molasses
3 tablespoons dark corn syrup
3 tablespoons ground ginger
3 tablespoons ground cinnamon
1 teaspoon ground cloves
1⅛ cups salted butter, cold and diced
1 teaspoon baking soda
4 cups all-purpose flour, plus extra for dusting
½ quantity royal icing (see pages 182–3)

equipment

Basic baking kit (see page 172)
Selection of townhouse, snowflake, and
gingerbread man and woman cookie cutters
Small electric drill with drill bit for food use
only, approximately ¼" diameter
Laser-cut townhouse stencils
Paper pastry bag (see page 184)
Mini candy canes (optional)
Red gingham ribbon, for hanging

Preheat the oven to 400 degrees F. Line two cookie sheets with waxed paper.

To make the gingerbread
Place the water, brown sugar, molasses, corn syrup, ground ginger, cinnamon, and cloves into a deep pan. Over medium heat, bring the mixture to a boil while stirring continuously. Remove from the heat, gradually add the diced butter, and stir until combined. Add the baking soda; take care as the mixture will swell up at this point. Let the mixture cool to room temperature.

Once cool, transfer the mixture to a large bowl. Sift in the flour and slowly mix together to form a slightly wet and sticky dough. Wrap in plastic wrap and chill for 2 hours or until cool and firm.

On a floured surface roll out the gingerbread dough to a thickness of approximately ¼". Using your selection of cookie cutters, cut out the various house, snowflake, man, and woman shapes and place them onto the prepared cookie sheets. Chill for at least 30 minutes.

Bake for 8 to 10 minutes, depending on size, or until the cookies spring back to the touch and are slightly darker around the edges.

To make the ribbon holes
Once the cookies are baked, remove from the oven and let cool completely. To make the ribbon holes, I use a small electric drill with a clean, sterilized drill bit. Place the cookie on a wire rack, then holding the electric drill vertically, make a small hole in the top of the cookie. This method prevents the cookie from breaking.

Alternatively, while the cookies are still hot, use a tiny round cookie cutter or the tip of a long thin pastry tip to make the ribbon holes. As the cookies are hot, take care not to burn your fingers when using this method.

STENCILING CAN APPEAR MORE DIFFICULT THAN IT REALLY IS. ONCE THE ICING TOUCHES THE COOKIE, IT WILL HELP TO HOLD THE STENCIL IN PLACE.

To ice the cookies

Following the instructions on page 182, prepare the royal icing, mixing it to a soft-peak consistency. Keep the icing covered with a damp cloth to prevent it from drying out.

To decorate the townhouse cookies, place a stencil on the surface of a cookie, holding it down at one end to prevent it from moving. Using a palette knife, scoop up a small amount of icing and spread it thinly over the stencil, ensuring that all gaps are covered. This appears trickier than it really is, as once the icing touches the stencil it helps to hold it in position. Carefully lift off the stencil and let the iced cookie dry. Clean the stencil before using it again.

To decorate the snowflake and gingerbread man and woman cookies, following the instructions on page 184, prepare a paper pastry bag. Fill the pastry bag with soft-peak consistency royal icing and cut a small section from the tip of the bag. Pipe the outlines and details onto each cookie as preferred. Use the same pastry bag to pipe an outline onto the townhouse cookies. While the icing is still wet, stick candy canes to the gingerbread man cookies.

Once all the cookies are decorated and dry, thread pieces of gingham ribbon through the holes. Hang the cookies on a tree to create a pretty winter village display.

tip

Humid or damp conditions can make gingerbread go soft. If the air is too dry, the icing can fall off.

THE SECRET TO PERFECTLY PIPED SWIRLS IS TO USE THE "LIFTING" METHOD DESCRIBED ON PAGE 185, IN WHICH THE PASTRY BAG HOVERS JUST ABOVE THE COOKIE.

MULLED WINE STARS

THIS SIMPLE YET DELICIOUS COOKIE RECIPE IS THE PERFECT CHRISTMAS COMFORT FOOD.
ENJOY THEM WITH A GLASS OF MULLED WINE (SEE PAGE 168).
ALTERNATIVELY, THESE TREATS CAN BE FLAVORED WITH SPICED ORANGE MARMALADE.

Makes approximately 20 cookies

ingredients

1⅛ cups unsalted butter, softened
1¼ cups superfine sugar
1 teaspoon ground cinnamon
Pinch of salt
1 large egg
3½ cups all-purpose flour,
plus extra for dusting
Confectioners' sugar, for dusting
1 cup Peggy's Mulled Wine Jam
or any other good-quality spiced
berry jam

equipment

Basic baking kit (see page 172)
One large and one small star
cookie cutter

Preheat the oven to 347 degrees F. Line a cookie sheet with waxed paper.

To make the cookies
Place the butter, sugar, cinnamon, and salt in a mixing bowl and cream together until smooth and creamy in texture.

Beat the egg lightly in another bowl and slowly add to the butter mixture while whisking until well incorporated.

Sift in the flour and mix until the dough just comes together. Gather the dough into a ball, wrap in plastic wrap, and chill for at least 30 minutes or until the dough feels firm and cool.

Place the dough on a floured surface and knead briefly.

Roll out the dough to a thickness of approximately ⅛ to ⅙". Using a large star cookie cutter, cut out 30 star shapes and place them onto the prepared cookie sheet.

Using a small star cookie cutter, cut the centers from 15 of the star shapes. You can reuse the cutout dough to make a few more stars. Chill again for 30 minutes or until cool and firm.

Bake for 6 minutes or until golden brown around the edges.

Once the cookies are baked, let them rest for about 30 minutes outside of the oven.

To assemble the cookies
Gently heat the jam in a pan until smooth. Spread one teaspoonful of jam evenly over the whole stars.

Lightly dust the hollow stars with confectioners' sugar and place one on top of each of the whole stars spread with jam.

CUPCAKE HEAVEN

BANOFFEE CUPCAKES

A FAVORITE AT THE PARLOUR, THIS RECIPE IS A FUSION OF BANANA SPLIT
AND BANOFFEE PIE. A DELICIOUS COMBO OF VANILLA SPONGE
WITH CHUNKY CHOCOLATE CHIPS AND FLUFFY FROSTING, THE SECRET LIES IN THE
SURPRISE FILLING OF CREAMY TOFFEE AND CHOPPED BANANAS.

Makes approximately 24 cupcakes

ingredients

For the decoration
5¾ ounces white sugar florist paste
Small amount of white vegetable fat
Brown and yellow paste food colour
Small amount of royal icing (see pages 182–3)

For the frosting
Generous ¾ cup regular cream cheese
Scant 1 cup unsalted butter, softened
4⅓ cups confectioners' sugar, sifted
1¾ ounces frozen banana puree (or make
your own by mashing a fresh banana)

For the sponge
Scant 1 cup unsalted butter, softened
1 cup superfine sugar
Pinch of salt
Seeds of 1 vanilla bean
4 medium eggs
Scant 1½ cups self-rising flour
2½ ounces semisweet chocolate (minimum
53% cocoa solids), chopped into small pieces

For the sugar syrup
⅔ cup water
¾ cup superfine sugar
Scraped vanilla bean

For the filling
7 ounces dulce de leche or soft caramel
(or make your own by boiling
a can of sweetened condensed milk
submerged in water for 3 hours)
1 large ripe banana

equipment

Basic baking kit (see page 172)
Small nonstick plastic board
Five-petal blossom cutter and veiner
Paper pastry bag (see page 184)
Paint palette or perforated foam pad,
to dry blossoms
Two 12-hole muffin trays
24 large brown cupcake cases
Melon baller
Plastic pastry bags
Large plain round piping tip

To make the decoration

Following the instructions on page 174, make the sugar blossom decorations one day ahead of assembling and serving. Make one blossom per cupcake.

Mix the sugar florist paste with a small amount of vegetable fat and the brown paste food color to a chocolate brown shade. Mix the royal icing with the yellow paste food color following the instructions on pages 182–3. Using a blossom cutter and veiner, make 24 sugar blossoms then pipe a yellow center into each flower. Let dry.

Preheat the oven to 347 degrees F. Prepare the muffin trays by placing the cupcake cases inside the holes.

To make the frosting

Place the cream cheese in a mixing bowl and beat until smooth and creamy.

Place the butter and confectioners' sugar in a separate mixing bowl. Reserve the vanilla bean for the sugar syrup. Cream together until very pale and fluffy.

Add the cream cheese, a little at a time, to the butter mixture and mix at medium–high speed until the frosting is combined. Add the banana puree. Chill until set.

To make the cupcakes

Place the butter, sugar, salt, and vanilla seeds in a mixing bowl and cream together until pale and fluffy.

Beat the eggs lightly in another bowl and slowly add to the butter mixture while whisking quickly. If the mixture starts to separate or curdle, stop adding the egg and beat in 2–3 tablespoons of flour. This will rebind the batter.

Once all the egg has been incorporated into the butter mixture, sift in the remaining flour and stir until the batter is just combined. This will ensure the sponges stay light and fluffy. Fold the chopped chocolate through the batter using a rubber spatula.

Using a plastic pastry bag or a tablespoon, carefully place the batter into the cupcake cases until two-thirds full only.

Bake for 12 to 15 minutes, depending on your oven. The cupcakes are cooked when the tops are golden brown and spring back to the touch. If in doubt, insert a clean knife or wooden skewer into the center of each sponge; it should come out clean.

To make the sugar syrup

While the cupcakes are baking, prepare the sugar syrup for soaking. Place the water, sugar, and vanilla bean into a pan and bring to a boil. Simmer until all the sugar crystals have dissolved. Set aside to cool down slightly. Discard the vanilla bean.

Once the cupcakes are baked, let them rest for about 10 minutes outside of the oven. Using a pastry brush, soak the tops of the cupcakes with sugar syrup while they are still warm; this allows the syrup to be absorbed faster.

Once warm, remove the cupcakes from the trays and let cool completely on a wire rack.

Once cool, wrap the cupcakes in plastic wrap and then chill for 1 hour or until the sponge feels firm to the touch. Using a melon baller, scoop out the tops of each cupcake.

To add the filling

Using a fork, crush the ripe banana and then mix it together with the dulce de leche. Place the banoffee mixture into a plastic piping bag and use to fill the scooped-out holes of the cupcakes.

To decorate

Following the instructions on page 178, prepare a plastic pastry bag fitted with a large plain round tip. Fill with the chilled frosting. Pipe a swirl of frosting on top of each cupcake.

To finish, place a sugar blossom on the top of the frosting for each cupcake.

STICKY TOFFEE CUPCAKES

THIS IS THE PARLOUR'S MOST POPULAR CUPCAKE. DUE TO THE GOOEY CARAMEL CENTER, THIS CAKE IS VERY MOIST. ITS DESSERT-LIKE TEXTURE MAKES IT THE PERFECT COMFORT FOOD FOR COLD AND RAINY FALL DAYS.

Makes approximately 24 cupcakes

ingredients

For the decoration
About 9 ounces marzipan
Small amount of white vegetable fat
Small amount of edible copper
and gold luster powder

For the frosting
Generous ¾ cup regular cream cheese
Scant 1 cup unsalted butter, softened
4⅓ cups confectioners' sugar, sifted
4½ ounces dulce de leche or soft caramel
(or make your own by boiling
a can of sweetened condensed milk
submerged in water for 3 hours)

For the cake batter
Generous ¼ cup water
10 ounces dates, pitted and roughly chopped
1½ teaspoons vanilla extract
Generous ½ cup unsalted butter, softened
Scant 1¼ cups soft brown sugar
2 cups self-rising flour
1½ teaspoons baking soda
3 large eggs
1½ cups walnuts, chopped and toasted

For the sugar syrup
⅔ cup water
¾ cup superfine sugar

For the filling
Approximately 9 ounces dulce de leche
or soft caramel (see above)

equipment

Basic baking kit (see page 172)
Fall leaf silicone mold
(I use a mold from First Impressions)
Large soft brush
Paint palette or perforated foam pad,
to dry leaves
Two 12-hole muffin trays
24 large brown cupcake cases
Plastic pastry bags
Large plain round piping tip

To make the decoration
Following the instructions on page 177, make the fall leaf decorations at least one day ahead of assembling and serving. Make one leaf per cupcake.

Preheat the oven to 347 degrees F. Prepare the muffin trays by placing the cupcake cases inside the holes.

To make the frosting
Place the cream cheese in a mixing bowl and beat until smooth and creamy.

Place the butter and confectioners' sugar in a separate mixing bowl and cream together until very pale and fluffy.

Add the cream cheese, a little at a time, to the butter mixture and mix at medium-high speed until the frosting is combined. Add the dulce de leche. Chill until set.

To make the cupcakes
Place the chopped dates into a mixing bowl and pour over the boiling water. Let soak for 20 minutes.

USING A PLAIN ROUND TIP, PIPE A PERFECT SWIRL OF FROSTING ON TO THE TOP OF EACH CUPCAKE BEFORE ADDING THE FINISHING DECORATIONS.

Once soaked, drain the dates and then gently break them up into smaller pieces. Add the vanilla extract to the dates.

Place the butter and sugar in a mixing bowl and cream together until pale and fluffy.

Sift the flour and baking soda into a separate bowl and set aside.

Whisk the eggs lightly in another bowl and slowly stir into the butter mixture. If the mixture starts to separate or curdle, stop adding the egg and beat in 2–3 tablespoons of the flour. This will rebind the batter.

Once all the egg has been incorporated into the butter mixture, fold in the remaining flour using a rubber spatula, followed by the soaked dates and chopped walnuts. Stir until the batter is just combined. This will ensure the sponges stay light and fluffy.

Using a plastic pastry bag or a tablespoon, carefully place the batter into the cupcake cases until two-thirds full only.

Bake for 15 to 20 minutes, depending on your oven. The cupcakes are cooked when the tops are golden brown and spring back to the touch. If in doubt, insert a clean knife or wooden skewer into the center of each sponge; it should come out clean.

To make the sugar syrup
While the cupcakes are baking, prepare the sugar syrup for soaking. Place the water and superfine sugar into a pan and bring to a boil. Simmer until all the sugar crystals have dissolved. Set aside to cool down slightly.

Once the cupcakes are baked, let them rest for about 10 minutes outside of the oven. Using a pastry brush, soak the tops of the cupcakes with sugar syrup while they are still warm; this allows the the syrup to be absorbed faster.

Once warm, remove the cupcakes from the trays and let cool completely on a wire rack.

Once cool, wrap the cupcakes in plastic wrap and then chill for 1 hour or until the sponge feels firm to the touch. Using a melon baller, scoop out the tops of each cupcake.

To add the filling
Place the dulce de leche into a plastic pastry bag and use to fill the scooped-out holes of the cupcakes.

To decorate
Following the instructions on page 178, prepare a plastic pastry bag fitted with a large plain round tip. Fill with the chilled frosting. Pipe a swirl of frosting on top of each cupcake.

To finish, place a marzipan leaf on the top of the frosting for each cupcake.

BLACK FOREST CUPCAKES

INSPIRED BY MY GERMAN ORIGINS, I HAVE TWEAKED THE CLASSIC BLACK FOREST GATEAÛX AND TURNED IT INTO A SUMPTUOUS CUPCAKE RECIPE. THE KEY IS TO USE PROPER "GRIOTTINES" CHERRIES, WHICH ARE WILD MORELLO CHERRIES, SOAKED IN KIRSCH LIQUEUR. THEY TASTE HEAVENLY—PLUMP, JUICY, AND VERY BOOZY.

Makes approximately 24 cupcakes

 ingredients

For the decoration
About 5½ ounces white sugar florist paste
Pink and brown paste food color
Small amount of royal icing (see pages 182–3)
Small amount of white vegetable fat
For the frosting
Generous ¾ cup regular cream cheese
Scant 1 cup unsalted butter
4⅓ cups confectioners' sugar, sifted
Small amount of Kirsch syrup, drained
from the cherries (see below)
For the cake mix
4½ ounces semisweet chocolate (minimum
53% cocoa solids), chopped or buttons
Scant ¾ cup milk
Scant 1½ cups light brown sugar
½ cup unsalted butter, softened
2 large eggs
Generous 1¼ cups all-purpose flour
Pinch of salt
½ teaspoon baking powder
½ teaspoon baking soda
1 heaping teaspoon unsweetened cocoa
powder
12 ounces Griottine cherries in Kirsch syrup
For the sugar syrup
⅔ cup water
¾ cup superfine sugar
Small amount of Kirsch syrup, drained
from the cherries (see above)
Scant ¼ cup Kirsch liqueur

equipment

Basic baking kit (see page 172)
Small nonstick plastic board
Medium and small five-petal blossom cutter
Blossom veiner
Paint palette or perforated foam,
to dry blossoms
Paper pastry bag (see page 184)
Two 12-hole muffin trays
24 large brown cupcake cases
Plastic pastry bags
Large star piping tip

To make the decoration
Following the instructions on page 174, make the sugar cherry blossom decorations at least one day ahead of assembling and serving. Make two or three blossoms per cupcake.

Mix the sugar florist paste with a small amount of pink paste food color to make a fuchsia shade. Mix the royal icing with the brown paste food color following the instructions on pages 182–3. Using a blossom cutter and veiner, make approximately 72 sugar blossoms then pipe a brown center into each flower. Let dry.

Preheat the oven to 347 degrees F. Prepare the muffin trays by placing the cupcake cases inside the holes.

To make the frosting
Place the cream cheese in a mixing bowl and beat until smooth and creamy. Place the butter and confectioners' sugar in a separate mixing

USING A STAR-SHAPED TIP, PIPE SWIRLS OF FROSTING OVER THE TOPS OF EACH CUPCAKE ENDING WITH A PERFECT PEAK.

bowl and cream together until very pale and fluffy. Add the cream cheese, a little at a time, to the butter mixture and mix at medium-high speed until the frosting is combined.

Flavor to taste with a few drops of the Kirsch syrup, making sure the frosting doesn't become too runny. Chill until set.

To make the cupcakes
Place the chocolate, milk, and half the sugar into a pan. Gently bring to a boil while stirring.

Place the butter and remaining sugar in a mixing bowl and cream together until very pale and fluffy.

Beat the eggs lightly in another bowl and slowly stir into the butter mixture.

Sift the flour, baking powder, baking soda, and cocoa powder into the batter and mix until just combined.

Slowly pour the hot chocolate into the batter and mix. Scrape the bowl with a rubber spatula to make sure the batter is well combined. Transfer the batter to a measuring cup or pitcher.

While still warm. pour the batter into the cupcake cases until two-thirds full only. Drop 2 or 3 griottine cherries into each cupcake.

Bake immedlately for 15   to 20 minutes, depending on your oven. The cupcakes are cooked when the tops spring back to the touch. If you insert a clean knife or wooden skewer into the center of the sponge, it should come out with a small amount of crumb sticking to it.

To make the sugar syrup
While the cupcakes are baking, prepare the sugar syrup for soaking. Place the water and superfine sugar into a pan and bring to a boil. Simmer until all the sugar crystals have dissolved. Set aside to cool down slightly. Flavor with some of the Kirsch syrup and Kirsch liqueur.

As soon as the cupcakes are baked, take them out of the oven. Using a pastry brush, soak the tops of the cupcakes with sugar syrup while they are still hot; this allows the syrup to be absorbed faster and prevent it from forming a crusty top.

Remove the cupcakes from the cookie sheets and let cool completely on a wire rack.

To decorate
Following the instructions on page 178, prepare a plastic pastry bag fitted with a large star tip. Fill with the chilled frosting. Pipe a rosette of frosting on top of each cupcake.

To finish, place 2 or 3 sugar blossoms on the top of the frosting for each cupcake.

STRAWBERRY AND CHAMPAGNE CUPCAKES

A SOPHISTICATED AND DELECTABLE CUPCAKE RECIPE,
PERFECT FOR A GARDEN PARTY IN THE BRITISH SUMMER.
ENJOY WITH A GLASS OF PINK CHAMPAGNE.

Makes approximately 24 cupcakes

ingredients

For the frosting
Generous ¾ cup regular cream cheese
Scant 1 cup unsalted butter, softened
4⅓ cups confectioners' sugar, sifted
Marc de Champagne, to taste
Pink paste food color
For the cake batter
Scant 1 cup unsalted butter, softened
1 cup superfine sugar
Pinch of salt
Seeds of 1 vanilla bean
4 medium eggs
Scant 1½ cups self-rising flour
For the syrup
⅔ cup water
¾ cup superfine sugar
Marc de Champagne, to taste
For the filling
About 1 cup Peggy's Strawberry
& Champagne Jam or any
other good-quality strawberry jam
For the decoration
12 small strawberries

equipment

Basic baking kit (see page 172)
Two 12-hole muffin trays
24 large silver cupcake cases
Plastic pastry bags
Large star piping tip

Preheat the oven to 347 degrees F. Prepare the muffin trays by placing the cupcake cases inside the holes.

To make the frosting
Place the cream cheese in a mixing bowl and beat until smooth and creamy.

Place the butter and confectioners' sugar in a separate mixing bowl and cream together until very pale and fluffy.

Add the cream cheese, a little at a time, to the butter mixture and mix at medium-high speed until the frosting is combined.

Flavor to taste with the Marc de Champagne, making sure the frosting doesn't become too runny. Add a small amount of pink paste food color and mix to a pale pastel shade. Chill in the refrigerator until set.

To make the cupcakes
Place the butter, sugar, salt, and vanilla seeds in a mixing bowl and cream together until pale and fluffy.

Beat the eggs lightly in another bowl and slowly pour into the butter mixture while whisking quickly. If the mixture starts to separate or curdle, stop adding the egg and beat in 2–3 tablespoons of flour. This will rebind the batter.

Once all the egg has been incorporated into the butter mixture, sift in the flour and stir until the batter is just combined. This will ensure the sponges stay light and fluffy.

Using a plastic pastry bag or a tablespoon, carefully place the batter into the cupcake cases until two-thirds full only.

Bake for 12 to 15 minutes, depending on your oven. The cupcakes are cooked when the tops are golden brown and spring back to the touch. If in doubt, insert a clean knife or wooden skewer into the center of each sponge; it should come out clean.

To make the sugar syrup
While the cupcakes are baking, prepare the sugar syrup for soaking. Place the water and superfine sugar into a pan and bring to a boil. Simmer until all the sugar crystals have dissolved. Set aside to cool. Once cool, flavor to taste with the Marc de Champagne.

Once the cupcakes are baked, let them rest for about 10 minutes outside of the oven. Using a pastry brush, soak the tops of the cupcakes with sugar syrup while they are still warm; this allows the syrup to be absorbed faster.

Once just warm, remove the cupcakes from the muffin trays and let cool completely on a wire rack.

Once cool, wrap the cupcakes in plastic wrap and then chill for 1 hour or until the sponge feels firm to the touch. Using a melon baller, scoop out the tops of each cupcake.

To add the filling
Using a teaspoon, fill the scooped-out holes of the cupcakes with the strawberry jam.

To decorate
Wash and cut the strawberries in half.

Following the instructions on page 178, prepare a plastic pastry bag fitted with a star tip. Fill with the chilled frosting. Pipe a rosette of frosting on top of each cupcake.

To finish, place a strawberry half on the top of the frosting for each cupcake.

LEMON AND RASPBERRY CUPCAKES

THIS IS A VERY SIMPLE AND LIGHT CUPCAKE THAT TASTES REFRESHING ON A SUMMER'S DAY. THE COMBINATION OF LEMON AND RASPBERRY CREATES A PERFECT BALANCE AND CUTS THROUGH THE SWEET CREAM CHEESE FROSTING.

Makes approximately 24 cupcakes

ingredients

For the frosting
Generous ¾ cup regular cream cheese
Scant 1 cup unsalted butter, softened
4⅓ cups confectioners' sugar, sifted
Finely grated zest of 2 unwaxed lemons

For the sponge
Scant 1 cup unsalted butter, softened
1 cup superfine sugar
Pinch of salt
Finely grated zest of 2 lemons
4 medium eggs
Scant 1½ cups self-rising flour
Carton of raspberries, plus extra for
the decoration

For the sugar syrup
⅔ cup freshly squeezed lemon juice
¾ cup superfine sugar

equipment

Basic baking kit (see page 172)
Two 12-hole muffin trays
24 large brown cupcake cases
Plastic pastry bags
Large round piping tip

Preheat the oven to 347 degrees F. Prepare the muffin trays by placing the cupcake cases inside the holes.

To make the frosting
Place the cream cheese in a mixing bowl and beat until smooth and creamy. Place the butter, confectioners' sugar, and lemon zest in another bowl and cream until very pale and fluffy. Add the cream cheese, a little at a time, to the butter and mix at medium-high speed until the frosting is combined. Chill until set.

To make the cupcakes
Place the butter, sugar, salt, and lemon zest in a mixing bowl and cream together until pale and fluffy. Beat the eggs lightly in another bowl and slowly pour into the butter mixture while whisking quickly. If the mixture starts to separate or curdle, stop adding the egg and beat in 2–3 tablespoons of the flour. This will rebind the batter. Once all the egg has been incorporated into the butter mixture, sift in the flour and stir until the batter is just combined. This ensures the sponges stay light and fluffy.

Using a pastry bag or tablespoon, place the batter into the cupcake cases until two-thirds full. Drop 2 or 3 raspberries into each cupcake.

Bake for 12 to 15 minutes, depending on your oven. The cupcakes are cooked when the tops are golden brown and spring back to the touch. If in doubt, insert a clean knife or wooden skewer into the center of each sponge; it should come out clean.

To make the sugar syrup
While the cupcakes are baking, prepare the sugar syrup for soaking. Place the lemon juice and superfine sugar into a pan and bring to a boil. Simmer until all the sugar crystals have dissolved. Set aside to cool down slightly.

Once the cupcakes are baked, let them rest for about 10 minutes outside of the oven. Using a pastry brush, soak the tops of the cupcakes with sugar syrup while they are still warm; this allows the syrup to be absorbed faster. Once warm, remove the cupcakes from the trays and let cool on a wire rack.

To decorate
Following the instructions on page 178, prepare a plastic pastry bag fitted with a large round tip. Fill with the chilled frosting. Pipe a swirl of frosting on top of each cupcake. To finish, place a raspberry on the top of the frosting for each cupcake.

VANILLA CHIFFON CUPCAKES

THIS IS A VERY LIGHT AND FLUFFY RECIPE USING REAL VANILLA AND CREAM CHEESE FROSTING. THE BEAUTY IS IN ITS SIMPLICITY AND PURITY OF FLAVORS. LESS IS SOMETIMES MORE…

Makes approximately 24 cupcakes

ingredients

For the decoration
1¾ ounces white sugar florist paste
Small amount of white vegetable fat
Small amount of royal icing (see pages 182–3)
Yellow paste food color

For the frosting
Generous ¾ cup regular cream cheese
Scant 1 cup unsalted butter, softened
4⅓ cups confectioners' sugar, sifted
Seeds of ½ vanilla bean
Yellow, orange, and teal paste food color

For the sponge
Scant 1 cup unsalted butter, softened
1 cup superfine sugar
Pinch of salt
Seeds of ½ vanilla bean
4 medium eggs
Scant 1½ cups self-rising flour

For the sugar syrup
⅔ cup water
¾ cup superfine sugar
Scraped vanilla bean

equipment

Basic baking kit (see page 172)
Small nonstick plastic board
Small five-petal blossom cutter and veiner
Paint palette or perforated foam pad, to dry blossoms
Paper pastry bag (see page 184)
Two 12-hole muffin trays
24 large brown cupcake cases

To make the decoration
Following the instructions on page 174, make the sugar blossom decorations one day ahead of assembling and serving. Make one blossom per cupcake.

Mix the sugar florist paste with a small amount of vegetable fat. Mix the royal icing with the yellow paste food color following the instructions on pages 182–3. Using a blossom cutter and veiner, make 24 sugar blossoms

then pipe a yellow center into each flower. Let dry.

Preheat the oven to 347 degrees F. Prepare the muffin trays by placing the cupcake cases inside the holes.

To make the frosting
Place the cream cheese in a mixing bowl and beat until smooth and creamy.

USING A SMALL PALETTE KNIFE, PILE THE FROSTING ONTO THE TOPS OF EACH CUPCAKE AND THEN SMOOTH OVER .

Place the butter, confectioners' sugar, and vanilla seeds in a separate mixing bowl and cream together until very pale and fluffy.

Add the cream cheese, a little at a time, to the butter mixture and mix at medium-high speed until the frosting is combined. Chill until set.

To make the cupcakes
Place the butter, sugar, salt, and vanilla seeds in a mixing bowl and cream together until pale and fluffy.

Beat the eggs lightly in another bowl and slowly add to the butter mixture while whisking quickly. If the mixture starts to separate or curdle, stop adding the egg and beat in 2–3 tablespoons of flour. This will rebind the batter.

Once all the egg has been incorporated into the butter mixture, sift in the flour and stir until the batter is just combined. This will ensure the sponges stay light and fluffy.

Using a plastic pastry bag or a tablespoon, carefully place the batter into the cupcake cases until two-thirds full only.

Bake for 12 to 15 minutes, depending on your oven. The cupcakes are cooked when the tops are golden brown and spring back to the touch. If in doubt, insert a clean knife or wooden skewer into the center of each sponge; it should come out clean.

To make the sugar syrup
While the cupcakes are baking, prepare the sugar syrup for soaking. Place the water, sugar, and vanilla bean into a pan and bring to a boil. Simmer until all the sugar crystals have dissolved. Set aside to cool down slightly. Discard the vanilla bean.

Once the cupcakes are baked, let them rest for about 10 minutes outside of the oven. Using a pastry brush, soak the tops of the cupcakes with sugar syrup while they are still warm; this allows the syrup to be absorbed faster.

Once just warm, remove the cupcakes from the trays and let cool completely on a wire rack.

To decorate
Divide the frosting into three equal parts. Mix the first third with a small amount of yellow paste food color, the second with orange paste food color, and the third with teal paste food color.

Following the instructions on page 179, frost the cupcakes using a small palette knife.

To finish, place a sugar blossom on the top of the frosting for each cupcake.

CHOCOLATE HEAVEN CUPCAKES

THIS CUPCAKE TASTES REALLY HEAVENLY. IT IS RICH, CREAMY,
AND SMOOTH, YET NOT TOO HEAVY. MOST OF ALL, IT IS VERY CHOCOLATEY.
THIS RECIPE IS SO YUMMY, WE HAVE EVEN WON AN AWARD FOR IT!
Makes approximately 24 cupcakes

ingredients

For the frosting
Scant ⅔ cup whipping cream
5¾ ounces semisweet chocolate (minimum
53% cocoa solids), chopped or in buttons
1 tablespoon glucose
Generous ¾ cup regular cream cheese
Scant 1 cup salted butter, softened
4 cups confectioners' sugar, sifted
For the cake mix
4½ ounces semisweet chocolate (minimum
53% cocoa solids), chopped or buttons
¾ cup milk
Scant 1½ cups light brown sugar
Generous ½ cup unsalted butter, softened
2 large eggs
Generous 1¼ cups all-purpose flour
Pinch of salt
½ teaspoon baking powder
½ teaspoon baking soda
1 heaping teaspoon unsweetened cocoa
For the decoration
Sheets of rice paper
Edible luster spray in pearlized
pink, blue, and green

equipment

Basic baking kit (see page 172)
Two 12-hole muffin trays
24 large brown cupcake cases
Plastic pastry bag
Large star piping tip
24 pearlized scallop-edged cupcake wrappers
Flower paper punch
(available from craft stores)

To make the decoration
Following the instructions on page 175, make the rice paper blossom decorations. Make one rice paper blossom per cupcake.

Preheat the oven to 325 degrees F. Prepare the muffin trays by placing the cupcake cases inside the holes.

To make the frosting
Place the cream in a pan and bring to a bare simmer. Place the chocolate and glucose into a bowl and pour the hot cream over the top. Whisk together until smooth, shiny and all the chocolate has melted. Once combined, let set at room temperature; the ganache should have the consistency of soft butter.

Place the cream cheese in a mixing bowl and beat until smooth and creamy.

Place the butter and confectioners' sugar in a separate mixing bowl and cream together until very pale and fluffy.

Add the ganache, a little at a time, to the buttercream mixture and mix at medium-high speed until the frosting is combined.

Gently stir one-third of the chocolate buttercream into the cream cheese.

Slowly whisk the remaining buttercream and add the chocolate cream cheese in two batches. Take care not to overwork the frosting as it can split. Chill until set.

To make the cupcakes
Place the chocolate, milk, and half the sugar into a pan. Gently bring to a boil while stirring.

Place the butter and remaining sugar in a mixing bowl and cream together until very pale and fluffy.

Beat the eggs lightly in another bowl and slowly stir into the butter mixture.

Sift the flour, baking powder, baking soda, salt, and cocoa powder together and add to the batter in two batches. Slowly mix until just combined.

Slowly pour the hot chocolate into the batter and mix. Scrape the bowl with a rubber spatula to make sure the batter is well combined.

Transfer the batter to a measuring cup or pitcher.

While still warm, pour the batter into the cupcake cases until two-thirds full only.

Bake immediately for 12 to 15 minutes, depending on your oven. The cupcakes are cooked when tops spring back to the touch and the edges have shrunk away from the side. Once cooked, the texture of this sponge is slightly sticky and dense. If you insert a clean knife or wooden skewer into the center of the sponge, it should come out with a small amount of crumb sticking to it.

Once the cupcakes are baked let them rest for a few minutes outside of the oven. Once just warm, remove the cupcakes from the baking trays and let cool completely on a wire rack.

To decorate
Following the instructions on page 178, prepare a plastic pastry bag fitted with a large star tip. Fill with the chilled frosting. Pipe a rosette of frosting on top of each cupcake.

To finish, place each cupcake into a wrapper and press a rice paper blossom on the top of the frosting for each cupcake.

COSMO CUPCAKES

CUPCAKES AND COCKTAILS GO HAND IN HAND, AND THE COSMOPOLITAN LENDS ITSELF PERFECTLY AS INSPIRATION FOR THIS RECIPE. FOR PARTY FUN, SERVE IN COCKTAIL GLASSES OR STICK SHORT DRINKING STRAWS INTO THE FROSTING.

Makes approximately 24 cupcakes

ingredients

For the sponge
¾ cup dried cranberries
Cointreau liqueur, for soaking
Scant 1 cup unsalted butter, softened
1 cup superfine sugar
Pinch of salt
Finely grated zest of 2 oranges
4 medium eggs
Scant 1½ cups self-rising flour
For the frosting
Generous ¾ cup regular cream cheese
Scant 1 cup unsalted butter, softened
Pinch of salt
4⅓ cups confectioners' sugar, sifted
Finely grated zest of 2 oranges
A dash of Cointreau liqueur, to taste
For the sugar syrup
⅔ cup freshly squeezed orange juice
¾ cup superfine sugar
Scant ¼ cup Cointreau liqueur
For the decoration
Metallic pink sugar pearls

equipment

Basic baking kit (see page 172)
Plastic pastry bag
Two 12-hole muffin trays
24 large metallic pink cupcake cases
Large star piping tip

Soak the cranberries in Cointreau liqueur, cover with plastic wrap, and let infuse overnight.

Preheat the oven to 347 degrees F. Prepare the muffin trays by placing the cupcake cases inside the holes.

To make the frosting
Following the instructions given on page 73, make the frosting using orange zest. Flavor with Cointreau liqueur to taste. Chill until set.

To make the cupcakes
Place the butter, sugar, salt, and orange zest in a bowl and cream together until pale and fluffy. Beat the eggs lightly in another bowl and slowly add to the butter mixture while whisking quickly. If the mixture starts to separate or curdle, stop adding the egg and beat in 2–3 tablespoons of flour. This will rebind the batter. Once all the egg has been incorporated into the butter mixture, sift in the flour and stir until the batter is just combined. This will ensure the sponges stay light and fluffy.

Using a pastry bag or tablespoon, place the batter into the cupcake cases until two-thirds full only. Drain the cranberries, reserving the liquid to add to the sugar syrup. Divide the cranberries evenly and drop into the cupcakes.

Bake for 12 to 15 minutes, depending on your oven. The cupcakes are cooked when the tops are golden brown and spring back to the touch. If in doubt, insert a clean knife or wooden skewer into the center of each sponge; it should come out clean.

To make the sugar syrup
While the cupcakes are baking, prepare the sugar syrup for soaking. Place the orange juice and superfine sugar into a pan and bring to a boil. Simmer until all the sugar crystals have dissolved. Let cool slightly. Flavor with the reserved Cointreau liquid to taste.

Once the cupcakes are baked, let them rest for 10 minutes outside of the oven. Using a pastry brush, soak the tops of the cupcakes with sugar syrup while they are still warm; this allows the syrup to be absorbed faster. Once warm, remove the cupcakes from the trays and let cool on a wire rack.

To decorate
Following the instructions on page 178, prepare a plastic pastry bag fitted with a large star tip. Fill with the chilled frosting. Pipe a rosette of frosting on top of each cupcake. To finish, sprinkle pink sugar pearls over the frosting for each cupcake.

LUSCIOUS
LAYER CAKES

SUMMER BERRY CAKE

AN UTTERLY SCRUMPTIOUS RECIPE FOR THE SERIOUSLY SWEET-TOOTHED
COMBINING HEAVENLY LIGHT BUTTERCREAM,
FLUFFY VANILLA SPONGE, AND SWEET SUMMER BERRIES.

Makes one 6"-round cake, serving 8 to 12 slices

ingredients

For the sponge
Scant 1 cup unsalted butter, softened
1 cup superfine sugar
Pinch of salt
Seeds of 1 vanilla bean
4 medium eggs
Scant 1½ cups self-rising flour

For the sugar syrup
⅔ cup water
¾ cup superfine sugar
Scraped vanilla bean

For the buttercream filling
1⅛ cups unsalted butter, softened
2¼ cups confectioners' sugar, sifted
Pinch of salt
3 tablespoons Peggy's Summer Berry
Jam or any other good-quality mixed
berry jam

For the decoration
1 tablespoon unsweetened cocoa powder

equipment

Basic baking kit (see page 172)
Three 6"-round sandwich pans
Cake leveler or large serrated knife
Nonslip turntable
Flat disk to place on top of the turntable
(I use the loose base of a 12"-springform
cake pan)
Metal side scraper
Laser-cut damask cake stencil

Bake the sponges one day ahead of serving. Make the sugar syrup while baking the sponges. Prepare the buttercream filling and assemble and decorate the cake on the day of serving. Dust the cake with the cocoa powder immediately before serving as, after a few hours, the cocoa powder may absorb moisture from the buttercream and appear wet.

Preheat the oven to 347 degrees F.

Prepare the sandwich pans by greasing the sides and lining the bases with waxed paper. Place the pan on top of the waxed paper, draw a line around the base with a pencil, and use as a guide to cut out a disk to line the base. Place the waxed paper disks inside the pans.

To make the sponge
Place the butter, sugar, salt, and vanilla seeds into a bowl and cream together until pale.

Beat the eggs lightly in another bowl and slowly add to the butter mixture while whisking quickly. If the mixture starts to separate or curdle, stop adding the egg and beat in 2–3 tablespoons of the flour. This will rebind the batter. Once all the egg has been added and combined with the butter mixture, sift in the flour and fold through until the batter is just combined. This will ensure the sponges stay light and fluffy.

Divide the batter evenly between the cake pans. If you find it difficult to measure by eye, use your kitchen scales to weigh out the amount of sponge batter for each pan.

Bake for 15 to 20 minutes, depending on your oven. If you are using deeper cake pans, the sponges may take longer to cook. The sponges are cooked when the sides are beginning to shrink away from the edges of

TO DECORATE, CENTER THE STENCIL ON TOP OF THE CAKE AND DUST THE SURFACE WITH COCOA POWDER. LIFT THE STENCIL OFF THE CAKE.

the pans and the tops are golden brown and spring back to the touch. If in doubt, insert a clean knife or wooden skewer into the center of each sponge; it should come out clean.

To make the sugar syrup
While the sponges are baking, prepare the sugar syrup for soaking. Place the water, superfine sugar, and vanilla bean into a pan and bring to a boil. Simmer until all the sugar crystals have dissolved. Set aside to cool down slightly.

Once the sponges are baked, let them rest for about 10 minutes outside of the oven. Using a pastry brush, soak the tops of the sponges with syrup while they are still warm; this allows the syrup to be absorbed faster.

Once just warm, run a knife all the way around the sides of the pans, then remove the sponges from the pans, and let cool completely on a wire rack.

Once cool, wrap the sponges in plastic wrap and then rest them overnight at room temperature. This will ensure that all the moisture is sealed in and the sponges firm up to the perfect texture for trimming and layering. When trimmed too soon after baking, the sponges tend to crumble and may even break into pieces.

To make the buttercream filling
Place the butter, confectioners' sugar, and salt into a mixing bowl and cream together until very pale and fluffy.

Add the jam to the mixture and stir through until combined. If the jam is a little too firm or chunky to mix easily, warm it up in a microwave or pass it through a coarse strainer to remove any larger berries. Alternatively, blitz the jam in a blender.

To assemble the cake
Trim and sandwich together the three sponge layers using one-third of the buttercream filling. With the remaining buttercream filling, cover and mask the top and sides of the cake. For full instructions on how to do this, see pages 180–81.

To decorate
Center the damask cake stencil on the top of the masked cake. Dust the surface liberally with cocoa powder. Carefully lift the stencil off the cake to reveal the damask pattern.

Serve the cake at room temperature. This cake is best enjoyed within 3 days of baking, but it can last for up to 1 week.

tip

When making the sponges, use three shallow sandwich pans rather than one deep cake pan as the sponges will rise better and bake more evenly.

TIPSY ORANGE TRUFFLE CAKE

DELICIOUSLY FRAGRANT ORANGE SPONGE INFUSED WITH COINTREAU
AND LAYERED WITH SEMISWEET DARK CHOCOLATE GANACHE,
THIS PARLOUR FAVORITE IS THE ULTIMATE CHOCOLATE ORANGE RECIPE.
A VERY GROWN-UP, SERIOUSLY SMOOTH, AND YUMMY CAKE!

Makes one 6"-round cake, serving 8 to 12 slices

ingredients

For the sponge
Scant 1 cup unsalted butter, softened
1 cup superfine sugar
Pinch of salt
Finely grated zest of 3 oranges
4 medium eggs
Scant 1½ cups self-rising flour

For the sugar syrup
Juice of 3 freshly squeezed oranges
¾ cup superfine sugar
2 tablespoons Cointreau orange liqueur

For the ganache
Generous 1 cup whipping cream
10½ ounces semisweet chocolate (minimum
53% cocoa solids), chopped or in buttons
1 teaspoon glucose

For the filling
2 tablespoons Peggy's Orange & Cointreau
Marmalade or any other good-quality
orange marmalade

equipment

Basic baking kit (see page 172)
Three 6"-round sandwich pans
Large serrated knife or cake leveler
Nonslip turntable
Flat disk to place on top of the turntable
(I use the loose base of a 12"-
springform cake pan)
Metal side scraper
Paper pastry bag

Bake the sponges one day ahead of serving. Make the sugar syrup while baking the sponges. Prepare the filling and assemble and decorate the cake on the day of serving.

Preheat the oven to 347 degrees F.

Prepare the sandwich pans by greasing and lining them with waxed paper. For full instructions on how to do this, see page 87.

To make the sponge
Place the butter, sugar, salt, and orange zest into a mixing bowl and cream together until pale and fluffy.

Beat the eggs lightly in another bowl and slowly add to the butter mixture while whisking quickly. If the mixture starts to separate or curdle, stop adding the egg and beat in 2–3 tablespoons of the flour. This will rebind the batter. Once all the egg has been added and combined with the butter mixture, sift in the flour and stir until the batter is just combined. This will ensure the sponges stay light and fluffy.

Divide the batter evenly between the cake pans. If you find it difficult to measure by eye, use your kitchen scales to weigh out the amount of sponge batter for each pan.

Bake for 15 to 20 minutes, depending on your oven. If you are using deeper cake pans, the sponges will take longer to cook. The sponges are cooked when the sides are beginning to shrink away from the edges of the pans and the tops are golden brown and spring back to the touch. If in doubt, insert a clean knife or wooden skewer into the center of each sponge; it should come out clean.

To make the sugar syrup

While the sponges are baking, prepare the sugar syrup for soaking. Place the orange juice and superfine sugar into a pan and bring to a boil. Simmer until all the sugar crystals have dissolved. Set aside to cool down slightly and then add the orange liqueur.

Once the sponges are baked, let them rest for about 10 minutes outside of the oven. Using a pastry brush, soak the tops of the sponges with syrup while they are still warm; this allows the syrup to be absorbed faster.

Once just warm, run a knife all the way around the sides of the pans, remove the sponges from the pans, and let cool on a wire rack.

Once cool, wrap the sponges in plastic wrap and rest them overnight at room temperature. This will ensure that all the moisture is sealed in and the sponges firm up to the perfect texture for trimming and layering. When trimmed too soon after baking, the sponges tend to crumble and may even break into pieces.

To make the ganache

Place the cream in a pan and bring to a simmer. Place the chocolate in a bowl and pour over the hot cream. Gently stir with a whisk or spatula until the chocolate has melted. Add the glucose and let the ganache set until it has a butterlike consistency.

To assemble the cake

Trim and sandwich together the three sponge layers using 2 tablespoons of ganache for the first layer and 2 tablespoons of marmalade for the second layer. Using half of the remaining ganache, cover or crumb-coat the top and sides of the cake. For full instructions on how to do this, see pages 180–81.

To glaze the cake

Place the cake on a wire rack and slide a tray underneath. Reserve approximately 1 tablespoon of the ganache for piping the decoration, then warm the remaining ganache to a thick pouring consistency. Pour the warmed ganache over the top of the cake ensuring the sides are evenly covered. Tap the tray to spread out the ganache and pop any air bubbles that appear. Chill the cake until set.

To decorate

Place the cake on top of the turntable. Fill a paper pastry bag with the reserved ganache, snip a small hole from the tip of the bag and pipe a swag border around the circumference of the cake top, revolving the turntable as necessary.

Serve the cake at room temperature. This cake is best enjoyed within 3 days of baking, but it can last for up to 1 week.

LEMON LIMONCELLO CAKE

THIS IS A VERY LOVELY CAKE—LIGHT, MOIST, AND FULL OF FLAVOR.
A SCATTERING OF CUTE SUGAR DAISIES COMPLEMENTS THE REFRESHING
PALE LEMON BUTTERCREAM FROSTING.
Makes one 6"-round cake, serving 8 to 12 slices

ingredients

For the decoration
5½ ounces white sugar florist paste
Small amount of white vegetable fat
Green and yellow paste food color
Small amount of royal icing (see pages 182–3)

For the sponge
Scant 1 cup unsalted butter, softened
1 cup superfine sugar
Pinch of salt
Finely grated zest of 2 unwaxed lemons
4 medium eggs
Scant 1½ cups self-rising flour

For the sugar syrup
⅔ cup freshly squeezed lemon juice
¾ cup superfine sugar
Scant ¼ cup Limoncello liqueur

For the buttercream filling
Generous ⅓ cup unsalted butter
Scant ¾ cup confectioners' sugar, sifted
Pinch of salt
1½ tablespoons Peggy's Lemon Limoncello
Jelly or any other good-quality lemon jelly or
lemon curd

equipment

Basic baking kit (see page 172)
Three 6"-round sandwich pans
Cake leveler or large serrated knife
Nonslip turntable
Flat disk to place on top of the turntable
(I use the loose base of a 12"-
springform cake pan)
6"-round cake card
Metal side scraper
For the sugar daisies and leaves,
see the equipment list on page 173

Following the instructions on page 173, make the simple daisies and leaves decoration at least one day ahead of assembling and serving. Bake the sponges one day ahead of serving. Make the sugar syrup while baking the sponges. Prepare the filling and assemble and decorate the cake on the day of serving.

To make the decoration
Mix two-thirds of the sugar florist paste with a small amount of white vegetable fat. Mix the remaining third with the green paste food color to a pale green shade. Mix the royal icing with the yellow paste food color to a pale lemon shade following the instructions on page 182–3. Using a daisy plunge cutter, leaf cutter, and veiner, make approximately 12 simple sugar daisies and small leaves. Let set in a cool dry place.

Preheat the oven to 347 degrees F.

Prepare the sandwich pans by greasing and lining them with waxed paper. For full instructions on how to do this, see page 87.

To make the sponge
Place the butter, sugar, salt, and lemon zest into a mixing bowl and cream together until pale and fluffy.

Beat the eggs lightly in another bowl and slowly add to the butter mixture while whisking quickly. If the mixture starts to separate or curdle, stop adding the egg and beat in 2–3 tablespoons of the flour. This will rebind the batter. Once all the egg has been added and mixed with the butter mixture, sift in the flour and stir until the batter is just combined. This will ensure the sponges stay light and fluffy.

Divide the batter evenly between the sandwich pans. If you find it difficult to measure by eye, use your kitchen scales to weigh out the amount of sponge batter for each pan.

Bake for 15 to 20 minutes, depending on your oven. If you are using deeper cake pans, the sponges will take longer to cook. The sponges are cooked when the sides are beginning to shrink away from the edges of the pans and the tops are golden brown and spring back to the touch. If in doubt, insert a clean knife or wooden skewer into the center of each sponge; it should come out clean.

To make the sugar syrup
While the sponges are baking, prepare the sugar syrup for soaking. Place the lemon juice and superfine sugar in a pan and bring to a boil. Simmer until all the sugar crystals have dissolved. Set aside to cool down slightly and then add the Limoncello liqueur.

Once the sponges are baked, let them rest for about 10 minutes outside of the oven. Using a pastry brush, soak the tops of the sponges with syrup while they are still warm; this allows the syrup to be absorbed faster.

Once just warm, run a knife all the way around the sides of the pans, remove the sponges from the pans, and let cool completely on a wire rack.

Once cool, wrap the sponges in plastic wrap and rest them overnight at room temperature. This will ensure that all the moisture is sealed in and the sponges firm up to the perfect texture for trimming and layering. When trimmed too soon after baking, the sponges tend to crumble and may even break into pieces.

To make the buttercream filling
Place the butter, confectioners' sugar, and salt into a bowl and cream together until very pale and fluffy. Add the lemon jelly to the mixture and stir through until combined and smooth.

To assemble the cake
Trim and sandwich together the three sponge layers using one-third of the buttercream filling and the limoncello syrup for soaking. With the remaining buttercream filling, cover or mask the top and sides of the cake. For full instructions on how to do this, see pages 180–81. Chill until set.

To decorate
Arrange the sugar daisies and leaves around the circumference of the cake top and stick them down with a dab of buttercream.

Serve the cake at room temperature. This cake is best enjoyed within 3 days of baking, but it can last for up to 1 week.

tip

Decorations made from sugar can attract moisture and may collapse when exposed to humid conditions. Therefore, do not store the cake in the refrigerator once decorated if it is not being eaten on the same day.

CREAMY CARAMEL CAKE

A SUMPTUOUS RECIPE FOR LOVERS OF ALL THINGS SWEET. THE HINT OF BRANDY PERFECTLY COMPLEMENTS THE CARAMEL FLAVORS WHILE THE SCULPTED DESIGN AND COCOA DUSTING CREATE A COOL CONTEMPORARY LOOK.

Makes one 6"-round cake, serving 8 to 12 slices

ingredients

For the sponge
Scant 1 cup unsalted butter, softened
1 cup superfine sugar
Pinch of salt
Seeds of 1 vanilla bean
4 medium eggs
Scant 1½ cups self-rising flour

For the sugar syrup
⅔ cup water
¾ cup superfine sugar
Scraped vanilla bean
2 tablespoons brandy

For the buttercream filling
7 tablespoons unsalted butter
Scant 1 cup confectioners' sugar, sifted
Pinch of salt
1¾ ounces dulce de leche or a can of sweetened condensed milk boiled in water for 3 hours

For the decoration
2 tablespoons unsweetened cocoa powder

equipment

Basic baking kit (see page 172)
Three 6"-round sandwich pans
Cake leveler or large serrated knife
Nonslip turntable
Flat disk to place on top of the turntable
(I use the loose base of a 12"-springform cake pan)
6"-round cake card
Ridged side scraper (I use one from Wilton)

Bake the sponges one day ahead of serving. Make the sugar syrup while baking the sponges. Prepare the filling and assemble and decorate the cake on the day of serving. Dust the cake with the cocoa powder immediately before serving as, after a few hours, the cocoa powder may absorb moisture from the buttercream and appear wet.

Preheat the oven to 347 degrees F.

Prepare the sandwich pans by greasing and lining them with waxed paper. For full instructions on how to do this, see page 87.

To make the sponge
Place the butter, sugar, salt, and vanilla seeds in a mixing bowl and cream together until pale and fluffy.

Beat the eggs lightly in another bowl and slowly add to the butter mixture while whisking quickly. If the mixture starts to separate or curdle, stop adding the egg and beat in 2–3 tablespoons of flour. This will rebind the batter. Once all the egg has been added and combined with the butter mixture, sift in the flour and stir until the batter is just combined. This will ensure the sponges stay light and fluffy.

Divide the batter evenly between the cake pans. If you find it difficult to measure by eye, use your kitchen scales to weigh out the amount of sponge batter for each pan.

Bake for 15 to 20 minutes, depending on your oven. If you are using deeper cake pans, the sponges will take longer to cook. The sponges are cooked when the sides are beginning to

USE A RIDGED SIDE SCRAPER TO CREATE THE SCULPTED BARREL DESIGN AROUND THE CAKE. SMOOTH OVER THE TOP WITH A PALETTE KNIFE.

shrink away from the edges of the pans and the tops are golden brown and spring back to the touch. If in doubt, insert a clean knife or wooden skewer into the center of each sponge; it should come out clean.

To make the sugar syrup

While the sponges are baking, prepare the sugar syrup for soaking. Place the water, superfine sugar, and vanilla bean in a pan and bring to a boil. Simmer until all the sugar crystals have dissolved. Set aside to cool and then add the brandy.

Once the sponges are baked, let them rest for about 10 minutes outside of the oven. Using a pastry brush, soak the tops of the sponges with syrup while they are still warm; this allows the syrup to be absorbed faster.

Once just warm, run a knife all the way around the sides of the pans, remove the sponges from the pans, and let cool completely on a wire rack.

Once cool, wrap the sponges in plastic wrap and rest them overnight at room temperature. This will ensure that all the moisture is sealed in and the sponges firm up to the perfect texture for trimming and layering. When trimmed too soon after baking, the sponges tend to crumble and may even break into pieces.

To make the buttercream filling

Place the butter, confectioners' sugar, and salt into a mixing bowl and cream together until very pale and fluffy.

Add the dulce de leche to the mixture and stir through until combined and smooth.

To assemble the cake

Trim and sandwich together the three sponge layers using one-third of the buttercream filling and the brandy syrup for soaking. With the remaining buttercream filling, cover or mask the top and sides of the cake. For full instructions on how to do this, see pages 180–81.

To decorate

Cover the chilled cake with another generous layer of buttercream and, using a side-scraper with ridges, create a sculpted barrel design. If you are unable to achieve a perfect sculpted side on your first attempt, simply scrape off any excess buttercream and repeat the process until you are happy with the result, Clean up the top with a palette knife.

Chill until set. Dust the top of the cake liberally with cocoa powder before serving.

Serve the cake at room temperature. This cake is best enjoyed within 3 days of baking, but it can last for up to 1 week.

DARK CHOCOLATE TRUFFLE CAKE

THIS IS A RICH AND SMOOTH CHOCOLATE RECIPE THAT TASTES AT ITS BEST WHEN SERVED AT ROOM TEMPERATURE. THE GANACHE GLAZE HAS A MELT-IN-THE-MOUTH TEXTURE AND A SMELL THAT IS UTTERLY ADDICTIVE.

Makes one 6"-square cake, serving approximately 18 slices

ingredients

For the cake batter
9 ounces semisweet chocolate (minimum 53% cocoa solids), chopped or in buttons
Scant 1½ cups milk
Generous 2¾ cups soft light brown sugar
Scant 1 cup unsalted butter, softened
4 large eggs
Scant 2⅔ cups all-purpose flour
1 teaspoon baking powder
1 teaspoon baking soda
Pinch of salt
1 tablespoon unsweetened cocoa powder

For the ganache
Scant 1¼ cups whipping cream
12 ounces semisweet chocolate (minimum 53% cocoa solids), chopped or in buttons
1 ounce glucose

equipment

Three 6"-square sandwich pans
Cake leveler or large serrated knife
Nonslip turntable
Flat disk to place on top of the turntable (I use the loose base of a 12"-springform cake pan)
6"-square cake card
Metal side scraper
Plastic pastry bag
Metal star piping tip

Bake the sponge one day ahead of serving. Assemble and decorate the cake on the day of serving. Prepare the ganache filling a few hours before use, so it has time to set.

Preheat the oven to 325 degrees F.

Prepare the sandwich pans by greasing and lining them with waxed paper. For full instructions on how to do this, see page 87.

To make the cake
Place the chocolate, milk, and scant 1½ cups of the light brown sugar in a deep pan and bring to a boil, stirring with a spatula.

Place the butter and the remaining light brown sugar in a mixing bowl and cream together until pale and fluffy.

Beat the eggs lightly in another bowl and slowly add to the butter mixture while whisking quickly.

Sift the flour, baking powder, baking soda, salt, and cocoa powder together and add to the butter mixture in two batches. Mix together slowly until the batter is just combined.

Slowly pour the hot chocolate mix into the batter in a thin and steady stream, mixing at a medium speed. Scrape the bottom of the mixing bowl with a rubber spatula to make sure the batter is well combined.

Immediately pour the sponge batter into the lined cake pans and bake for 30 to 40 minutes, depending on your oven. The sponge is cooked when the sides are beginning to shrink away

TO DECORATE THE TOP EDGE, PIPE A SERIES OF S-SCROLLS AND C-SCROLLS. FOR THE BOTTOM EDGE, PIPE A BORDER OF SHELLS.

from the edges of the pan and the top springs back to the touch. Once cooked, the texture of this chocolate cake is slightly sticky and dense. If you insert a clean knife or wooden skewer into the center of the sponge, it should come out with a small amount of crumb sticking to it.

Once the sponge is baked, let it rest for about 30 minutes outside of the oven.

Once just warm, run a knife all the way around the sides of the pan, remove the cake from the pan, and let cool completely on a wire rack.

Once cool, wrap the sponge in plastic wrap and then rest it overnight at room temperature. This will ensure that all the moisture is sealed in and the sponge firms up to the perfect texture for trimming and layering. When trimmed too soon after baking, the sponge tends to crumble and may even break into pieces.

To make the ganache
Place the cream in a pan and bring to a bare simmer.

Place the chocolate and glucose into a bowl and pour the hot cream over the top. Whisk together until smooth. Once combined, let set at room temperature; the ganache should have the consistency of soft butter.

To assemble the cake
Using the cake leveler or serrated knife, trim the top and bottom crusts off the sponge. Slice the trimmed sponge into three horizontal layers of equal depth. Sandwich together the three sponge layers using the ganache. With

one-third of the ganache, cover or crumb-coat the top and sides of the cake. For full instructions on how to do this, see pages 180–81. Working with a square cake is slightly trickier than a round as you must cover each of the four sides separately. Chill until set.

To glaze the cake
Place the cake on a wire rack and slide a tray underneath. Warm the remaining ganache to a thick pouring consistency. Pour the warmed ganache over the top of the cake ensuring the sides are evenly covered. Tap the tray to spread out the ganache and pop any air bubbles that appear. Chill the cake until set.

To decorate
Place the cake either on a cakestand or on top of the turntable covered with a piece of waxed paper.

Take the ganache caught in the tray and whisk it by hand until it stiffens slightly. Place a star tip into a plastic pastry bag and fill with a small amount of the stiffened ganache. Pipe a border of S-scrolls and C-scrolls all around the edges of the cake top, Pipe a border of shells all around the bottom edge. For full instructions on how to do this, see page 185. If the cake has been placed on waxed paper, chill until the piped borders are set before transferring to a cakestand.

Serve the cake at room temperature. This cake is best enjoyed within 3 days of baking, but it can last for up to 1 week.

WHITE CHOCOLATE PASSION CAKE

THIS CAKE HAS AN EXOTIC FLAVOR COMBINATION. AT FIRST BITE,
YOU TASTE THE SWEETEST WHITE CHOCOLATE BUT THEN THE PUNCHY PASSION FRUIT
JAM BURSTS IN YOUR MOUTH. DECORATE WITH PIPED SWAGS AND
PRETTY CANDLES FOR A SIMPLE YET SOPHISTICATED BIRTHDAY CAKE.

Makes one 6"-round cake, serving approximately 12 slices

ingredients

For the cake batter
4½ ounces white chocolate, chopped or in buttons
¾ cup milk
Scant ⅓ cup soft light brown sugar
1⅛ cups superfine sugar
Scant ½ cup unsalted butter, softened
2 large eggs
1½ cups all-purpose flour
1 teaspoon baking powder
Pinch of salt

For the chocolate buttercream
Scant ¼ cup whipping cream
2½ ounces white chocolate, chopped or in buttons
4 tablespoons unsalted butter, softened
½ cup confectioners' sugar, sifted

For the filling
2 tablespoons Peggy's Passion fruit Jam or any other good-quality passion fruit jam

equipment

Basic baking kit (see page 172)
Three 6"-round sandwich pans
Cake leveler or large serrated knife
Nonslip turntable
Flat disk to place on top of the turntable
(I use the loose base of a 12"-springform cake pan)
6"-round cake card
Metal side scraper
Plastic pastry bag
Plain round ¼"-piping tip

Bake the sponges one day ahead of serving. Prepare the buttercream filling and assemble and decorate the cake on the day of serving.

Preheat the oven to 325 degrees F.

Prepare the sandwich pans by greasing and lining them with waxed paper. For full instructions on how to do this, see page 87.

To make the cake
Place the white chocolate, milk, light brown sugar, and scant ½ cup of the superfine sugar in a deep pan and bring to a boil, stirring with a spatula.

Place the butter and the remaining superfine sugar in a mixing bowl and cream together until pale and fluffy.

Beat the eggs lightly in another bowl and slowly add to the butter mixture while whisking quickly.

Sift the flour, baking powder, and salt together and add to the butter mixture in two batches. Mix together at a slow speed until the batter is just combined.

Slowly pour the hot chocolate mix into the batter in a thin and steady stream, mixing at a medium speed. Scrape the bottom of the mixing bowl with a rubber spatula to make sure the batter is well combined.

Immediately pour the sponge batter into the lined cake pans, dividing the batter evenly. If you find it difficult to measure by eye, use your kitchen scales to weigh out the amount of cake batter for each pan.

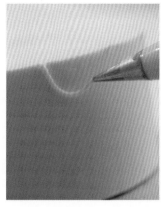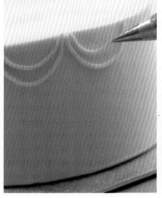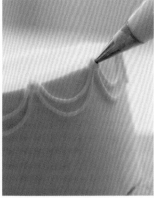

DIVIDE THE TOP EDGE INTO TWELVE EQUAL SEGMENTS, THEN PIPE A BORDER
OF DOUBLE SWAGS FINISHED OFF WITH DOTS.

Bake for 25 to 30 minutes, depending on your oven. If you are using deeper cake pans, the sponges will take longer to cook. The sponges are cooked when the sides are beginning to shrink away from the edges of the pans and the tops are golden brown and spring back to the touch. If in doubt, insert a clean knife or wooden skewer into the center of each sponge; it should come out clean.

Once the sponges are baked, let them rest for about 30 minutes outside of the oven. Once just warm, run a knife all the way around the sides of the pan, remove the cake from the pan, and let cool completely on a wire rack.

Once cool, wrap the sponges in plastic wrap and then rest it overnight at room temperature. This will ensure that all the moisture is sealed in and the sponges firm up to the perfect texture for trimming and layering. When trimmed too soon after baking, the sponges tend to crumble and may even break into pieces.

To make the chocolate buttercream

Place the cream in a pan and bring to a bare simmer.

Place the white chocolate in a bowl and pour the hot cream over the top. Whisk together until smooth. Once combined, let set at room temperature; the white chocolate ganache should have the consistency of soft butter.

Place the butter and confectioners' sugar in a mixing bowl and cream together until pale and fluffy. One spoonful at a time, add the white chocolate ganache to the mixture and stir through until well combined.

To assemble the cake

Trim and sandwich together the three sponge layers using the passion fruit jam. Reserve 1 tablespoon of the chocolate buttercream for the piped decoration, then with the remaining buttercream, cover or mask the top and sides of the cake. For full instructions on how to do this, see pages 180–81. Chill until set.

To decorate

Place the cake either on a cakestand or on top of the turntable covered with a piece of waxed paper.

Place a round tip into a plastic pastry bag and fill with the remaining buttercream. Divide the top of the cake into 12 equal segments. At the top edge, pipe a series of double swags all around the sides, revolving the turntable as necessary. To finish, pipe dots on top of the swag joints and pipe a row of dots all around the bottom edge of the cake. For full instructions on how to do this, see page 185. If the cake has been placed on waxed paper, chill until the piped dots are set before transferring to a cakestand.

Serve the cake at room temperature. This cake is best enjoyed within 3 days of baking, but it can last for up to 1 week.

SCRUMPTIOUS CARROT CAKE

AN EXCEPTIONALLY MOIST, PERFECTLY BALANCED CAKE BAKED WITH CHUNKS OF JUICY PINEAPPLE AS WELL AS CARROTS AND WALNUTS. WONDERFUL WITH LEMON BUTTERCREAM, IT CAN ALSO BE BAKED IN A LOAF PAN AND ENJOYED ON ITS OWN.

Makes one 6"-round cake, serving 8 to 12 slices

ingredients

For the cake batter
Scant ⅔ cup vegetable oil
1 cup light brown sugar
Generous ⅓ cup beaten eggs
(approximately 1½ small eggs)
¾ cup walnuts, toasted and finely chopped
11 ounces carrots, peeled and grated
10 ounces canned pineapple, crushed
2 cups all-purpose flour
¾ teaspoon baking soda
¾ teaspoon baking powder
¾ teaspoon ground cinnamon
Pinch of salt
Seeds of 1 vanilla bean

For the buttercream filling
9 tablespoons unsalted butter, softened
1 cup confectioners' sugar, sifted
Finely grated zest of a unwaxed lemon
Pinch of salt

For the decoration
5½ ounces white rolled fondant
1 teaspoon gum tragacanth
Small amount of white vegetable fat
Orange, green, blue, and brown
paste food color
Small amount of clear alcohol or edible glue

equipment

Basic baking kit (see page 172)
Three 6"-round sandwich pans
Cake leveler or large serrated knife
Nonslip turntable
Flat disk to place on top of the turntable
(I use the loose base of a 12"-
springform cake pan)
6"-round cake card
Metal side scraper
Plastic pastry bag
Plain round ¼"-piping tip
To make the appliqué blossoms, see the
equipment list on page 176

Bake the sponges one day ahead of serving. Prepare the buttercream filling and assemble and decorate the cake on the day of serving.

Preheat the oven to 350 degrees F.

Prepare the sandwich pans by greasing and lining them with waxed paper. For full instructions on how to do this, see page 87.

To make the cake
Place the vegetable oil and light brown sugar in a mixing bowl and beat together. Beat the eggs lightly in another bowl and gradually add to the oil mixture until you get a smooth emulsion. Add the walnuts, carrots, and pineapple and gently mix until well combined.

Sift the flour, baking soda, baking powder, ground cinnamon, and salt together and add to the wet mixture in two batches. Mix together at a slow speed until the batter is just combined.

Divide the batter evenly between the sandwich pans. If you find it difficult to measure by eye, use your kitchen scales to weigh out the amount of sponge batter for each pan.

Bake for 40 to 50 minutes, depending on your oven. If you are using deeper cake pans, the sponges will take longer to cook. The sponges are cooked when the sides are beginning to shrink away from the edges of the pans and the tops are golden brown and spring back to the touch. If in doubt, insert a clean knife or wooden skewer into the center of each sponge; it should come out clean.

MAKE APPLIQUÉ BLOSSOM DECORATIONS FROM ROLLED FONDANT IN AN ASSORTMENT OF COLORS, LAYERING DIFFERENT SIZES AND SHAPES TO MAKE EACH FLOWER.

Once the sponges are baked, let them rest for about 10 minutes outside of the oven. Once just warm, remove the sponges from the pans and let cool completely on a wire rack.

Once cool, wrap the sponges in plastic wrap and then rest overnight at room temperature. This will ensure that all the moisture is sealed in and the sponges firm up to the perfect texture for trimming and layering. When trimmed too soon after baking, the sponges tend to crumble and may even break into pieces.

To make the buttercream filling
Place the butter, confectioners' sugar, lemon zest, and salt in a mixing bowl and cream together until very pale and fluffy.

To assemble the cake
Trim and sandwich together the three sponge layers using one-third of the lemon buttercream filling. With the remaining buttercream filling, cover or mask the top and sides of the cake. For full instructions on how to do this, see pages 180–81. Chill until set.

To decorate
Following the instructions on page 176, make a selection of appliqué blossoms.

Place the cake either on to a cakestand or on top of the turntable covered with a piece of waxed paper.

Arrange the decorations around the sides of the cake and stick them down with a dab of buttercream. Trim away any overlap with a kitchen knife.

Place a round tip into a plastic pastry bag and fill with the remaining buttercream. Around the sides, pipe rows of dots in between the blossoms, revolving the turntable as necessary. To finish, pipe a border of shells all around the top and bottom edges of the cake. For full instructions on how to do this, see page 185. If the cake has been placed on waxed paper, chill until the piped borders are set before transferring to a cakestand.

Serve the cake at room temperature.

GLORIOUS VICTORIA CAKE

BASED ON A CLASSIC VICTORIA SPONGE, THE KEY TO THIS SIMPLY DELICIOUS CAKE'S
SUCCESS IS USING THE BEST QUALITY INGREDIENTS. FOR ADDED FLAVOR
AND MOISTURE, SOAK THE SPONGE LAYERS IN VANILLA SUGAR SYRUP.
THE DESIGN IS INSPIRED BY THE ERA OF THE CAKE'S ORIGIN, DECORATED USING
A VICTORIAN-STYLE SCROLL AND SHELL PIPING TECHNIQUE.

Makes one 6"-round cake, serving 8 to 12 slices

ingredients

For the sponge
Scant 1 cup unsalted butter, softened
1 cup superfine sugar
Pinch of salt
Seeds of ½ vanilla bean
4 medium eggs
Scant 1½ cups self-rising flour

For the sugar syrup
⅔ cup water
¾ cup superfine sugar
Scraped vanilla bean

For the buttercream filling
1⅓ cups unsalted butter, softened
Scant 2⅔ cups confectioners' sugar, sifted
Pinch of salt
Seeds of ½ vanilla bean
Small amount of pink food paste color
3 tablespoons good-quality raspberry jam

equipment

Three 6"-round sandwich pans
Cake leveler or large serrated knife
Nonslip turntable
Flat disk to place on top of the turntable
(I use the loose base of a 12"-
springform cake pan)
6"-round cake card
Metal side scraper
Two plastic pastry bags
Medium star piping tip
Plain round ¼"-piping tip

Bake the sponges one day ahead of serving. Make the sugar syrup while baking the sponges. Prepare the buttercream filling and assemble and decorate the cake on the day of serving.

Preheat the oven to 347 degrees F.

Prepare the sandwich pans by greasing and lining them with waxed paper. For full instructions on how to do this, see page 87.

To make the sponge
Place the butter, sugar, salt, and vanilla seeds in a mixing bowl and cream together until pale and fluffy.

Beat the eggs lightly in another bowl and slowly add to the butter mixture while whisking quickly. If the mixture starts to separate or curdle, stop adding the egg and beat in 2–3 tablespoons of the flour. This will rebind the batter. Once all the egg has been added and combined with the butter mixture, sift in the flour and stir until the batter is just combined. This will ensure the sponges stay light and fluffy.

Divide the batter evenly between the sandwich pans. If you find it difficult to measure by eye, use your kitchen scales to weigh out the amount of sponge batter for each pan.

Bake for 15 to 20 minutes, depending on your oven. If you are using deeper cake pans, the sponges will take longer to cook. The sponges are cooked when the sides are beginning to shrink away from the edges of the pans and the tops are golden brown and spring back to the touch. If in doubt, insert a clean knife or wooden skewer into the center of each sponge; it should come out clean.

IN RESPECT TO THE ORIGINS OF THIS CLASSIC SPONGE, DECORATE THE CAKE WITH A SELECTION OF VICTORIAN-STYLE PIPED SCROLLS.

To make the sugar syrup

While the sponges are baking, prepare the sugar syrup for soaking. Place the water, superfine sugar, and vanilla bean into a pan and bring to a boil. Simmer until all the sugar crystals have dissolved. Set aside to cool down slightly. Discard the vanilla bean.

Once the sponges are baked, let them rest for about 10 minutes outside of the oven. Using a pastry brush, soak the tops of the sponges with vanilla bean sugar syrup while they are still warm; this allows the syrup to be absorbed faster.

Once just warm, run a knife all the way around the sides of the pans, remove the sponges from the pans, and let cool completely on a wire rack.

Once cool, wrap the sponges in plastic wrap and then rest them overnight at room temperature. This will ensure that all the moisture is sealed in and the sponges firm up to the perfect texture for trimming and layering. When trimmed too soon after baking, the sponges tend to crumble and may even break into pieces.

To make the buttercream filling

Place the butter, confectioners' sugar, salt, and vanilla seeds into a mixing bowl and cream together until very pale and fluffy.

Add a small amount of pink food color to the mixture and stir through until combined and the buttercream is a pastel shade.

To assemble the cake

Trim and sandwich together the three sponge layers using one layer of buttercream filling and one layer of raspberry jam, and the vanilla sugar syrup for soaking. With the remaining buttercream filling, cover or mask the top and sides of the cake. For full instructions on how to do this, see pages 180–81.

To decorate

Place the cake either on to a cakestand or on top of the turntable covered with a piece of waxed paper.

Place a star tip into a plastic pastry bag and fill with a generous amount of the remaining buttercream. Place a round tip into another plastic pastry bag and fill with a small amount of the remaining buttercream.

Divide the top of the cake into eight equal segments. Using the star tip, pipe a ring of C-scrolls around the circumference, revolving the turntable as necessary. Next, pipe a shell from the middle of each C-scroll toward the center. Where all eight shells meet, pipe a rosette on top at the center of the cake top. Using the round tip, pipe a small dot between each shell.

Using the star tip, pipe eight fleur de lys evenly around the sides at the top edge, with a single upside-down shell underneath at the bottom edge. To finish, pipe a small dot between the fleur de lys and shell. For full instructions on how to do this, see page 185. If the cake has been placed on waxed paper, chill until the piped dots are set before transferring to a cakestand.

Serve the cake at room temperature. This cake is best enjoyed within 3 days of baking, but it can last for up to 1 week.

CLASSIC
CAKES & BAKES

NEAPOLITAN MARBLE CAKE

A DELICIOUS MARBLE CAKE BRINGS BACK FONDEST CHILDHOOD MEMORIES. IT NOT ONLY TASTES JUST LIKE THE ONE GRANDMA USED TO MAKE, BUT LOOKS VERY PRETTY INSIDE WHEN CUT. I HAVE REVIVED THIS RETRO CLASSIC BY ADDING A PALE PINK SPONGE SWIRL INTO THE MIX AND USING A TRADITIONAL BUNDT CAKE PAN IN A CONTEMPORARY SHAPE.

Makes one 12"-cake, serving 16 to 20 slices

ingredients

For the sponge
1⅛ cups unsalted butter, softened,
plus extra for greasing the cake pan
1¼ cups superfine sugar
Pinch of salt
Seeds of 1 vanilla bean
5 medium eggs
Generous 1¾ cups self-rising flour, sifted
¼ cup unsweetened cocoa powder
2 tablespoons milk
Pink liquid food color
All-purpose flour for dusting
Confectioners' sugar for dusting
For the sugar syrup
⅔ cup water
¾ cup superfine sugar

equipment

12"-Kugelhupf or Bundt cake pan

Preheat the oven to 347 degrees F. Prepare the cake pan by greasing with softened butter and dusting with all-purpose flour.

To make the sponge
Place the butter, superfine sugar, salt, and vanilla seeds in a mixing bowl and cream together until pale and fluffy.

Beat the eggs lightly in another bowl and slowly add to the butter mixture while whisking quickly. If the mixture starts to separate or curdle, stop adding the egg and beat in 2–3 tablespoons of the flour. This will rebind the batter.

Once all the egg has been added and combined with the butter mixture, sift in the flour and stir until the batter is just combined.

Divide the batter into three equal parts. Mix the first with a small amount of pink food color to create a pale pastel shade. Mix the second with the cocoa powder and add the milk. Keep the third plain.

Pour the pink batter into the bottom of the prepared cake pan, followed by the chocolate batter, and then finally the plain batter.

To "marble" the mixture, gently fold through all three colored layers with a fork or spatula.

Bake for approximately 1 hour, depending on your oven. If you are using a deeper cake pan, the sponge will take longer to cook. To check if the sponge is cooked, insert a clean knife or wooden skewer into the center of each sponge; it should come out clean.

To make the sugar syrup
While the sponge is baking, prepare the sugar syrup for soaking. Place the water and superfine sugar into a pan and bring to a boil. Simmer until all the sugar crystals have dissolved. Set aside to cool down slightly.

Once the sponge is baked, let it rest for approximately 10 minutes outside of the oven. Using a pastry brush, soak the tops of the sponges with sugar syrup while it is still warm; this allows the syrup to be absorbed faster.

Once just warm, remove the sponge from the pan and let cool completely on a wire rack.

Dust the top of the cake with confectioners' sugar before serving at room temperature.

CHOCOLATE HAZELNUT TORTE

DURING A TRIP TO THE AUSTRIAN CITY OF SALZBURG, I CAME ACROSS A CAKE THAT WAS SO MOIST, NUTTY, AND CHOCOLATEY, WITH A HINT OF RUM, THAT I COULDN'T GET ENOUGH OF IT. FOR ME IT WAS A SLICE OF CAKE HEAVEN, AN UNFORGETABLE EXPERIENCE THAT INSPIRED THIS RECIPE. I HOPE THAT YOU WON'T GET ENOUGH OF IT EITHER.

Makes one 8"-round cake, serving 8 to 12 slices

ingredients

For the torte

1 cup ground hazelnuts

2¾ ounces semisweet chocolate (minimum 53% cocoa solids), chopped or in buttons

Generous ⅓ cup self-rising flour

1 teaspoon ground cinnamon

11 tablespoons unsalted butter, softened

½ cup soft light brown sugar

Seeds of ½ vanilla bean

3 large eggs, separated

1½ tablespoons dark rum

Pinch of salt

Pinch of cream of tartar

1½ heaping tablespoons superfine sugar

For the decoration

9 ounces marzipan

9 ounces ganache (see page 105)

Confectioners' sugar for dusting

Unsweetened cocoa powder for dusting

equipment

8"-round springform cake pan

Flat metal tray or disk (I use the loose base of a large 12"-springform cake pan)

Large serrated knife

Large step palette knife

Laser-cut cake stencil with wheatsheaf or leaf pattern

Preheat the oven to 300 degrees F.

Prepare the springform cake pan by lining it with waxed paper. For full instructions on how to do this, see page 87.

To make the torte

Place the hazelnuts, chocolate, and flour in a food processor and grind until the mixture resembles coarse cookie crumbs, but is not oily. Transfer to a mixing bowl, add the ground cinnamon, and set aside.

Place the butter, light brown sugar, and vanilla seeds in a mixing bowl and cream together until pale and fluffy.

Beat the eggs yolks lightly in another bowl and slowly add to the butter mixture while whisking quickly until well incorporated.

Fold half the ground hazelnut and chocolate mixture into the batter. Add the rum, then fold in the other half.

In a clean dry bowl, whisk the egg whites with the salt and cream of tartar until they reach soft peaks. Add the superfine sugar and continue whisking until the meringue mixture is glossy but not dry.

Fold a tablespoonful of the meringue mixture into the batter to loosen it, then gently fold the rest in to keep the batter light.

Pour the batter into the prepared cake pan and level the surface using a palette knife or the back of a spoon.

Bake on a low shelf for 50 to 55 minutes, depending on your oven. The cake is cooked

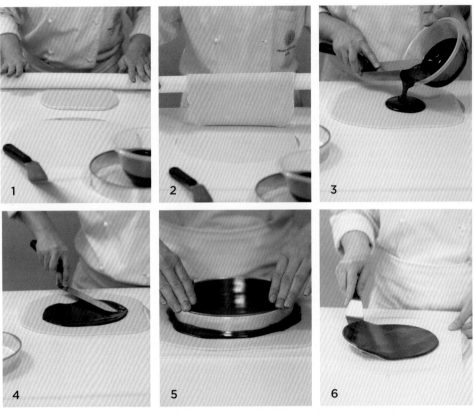

FOR THE FINISHING TOUCH TO THIS TORTE, ROLL OUT THE MARZIPAN TO A THIN SHEET THEN
POUR AND SPREAD THE GLOSSY GANACHE OVER THE TOP.

when the top is lightly browned and springs back to the touch. If in doubt, insert a clean knife or wooden skewer into the center of the cake; it should come out clean.

Once the cake is baked, let it rest for about 30 minutes outside of the oven. Once cool, remove the cake from the pan when you are ready to decorate.

To decorate
On a surface dusted with confectioners' sugar, roll the marzipan out to a thickness of ⅛ to ⅙" **(1)**. It must be large enough that you can cut a 8"-circle from it. Place the rolled marzipan on a flat metal tray or disk **(2)**.

Gently warm the ganache to a thick pouring consistency. Place the warmed ganache in a pitcher or bowl and tap the sides to release any air bubbles, which will rise to the top.

Slowly pour the ganache over the marzipan **(3)**. Using a large step palette knife, spread it out evenly across the marzipan **(4)**. If there are any air bubbles or lines, tap the metal tray to even out the surface. Chill in the refrigerator or freezer until the ganache has set.

If the top of the cake is uneven, level with a serrated knife and turn upside down so the perfectly flat side is facing upward. Brush the top of the cake with a thin layer of ganache.

Remove the marzipan and ganache sheet from the refrigerator. Carefully cut out a 8"-circle using a slightly warmed cutter **(5)**. Peel away any excess and use a step palette knife to gently lift and place the circle on top of the cake **(6)**.

While the ganache is still firm and set, center the stencil on the top of the ganache layer. Dust the surface liberally with cocoa powder. Carefully lift the stencil off the cake to reveal the pattern.

Serve the cake at room temperature.

LEMON, ALMOND, AND POPPY SEED CAKE

A LIGHT AND ZINGY CAKE SPECKLED WITH POPPY SEEDS, WHICH NOT ONLY LOOK PRETTY BUT ALSO ADD A BIT OF CRUNCH TO THE TEXTURE. A DELICIOUSLY MOIST SPONGE, THIS CAKE WILL LAST FOR A FEW DAYS WHEN KEPT AT ROOM TEMPERATURE.

Makes one 10"-cake, serving 12 to 16 slices

ingredients

For the sponge
Scant 1 cup unsalted butter, softened, plus extra for greasing the cake pan
All-purpose flour for dusting
1 cup superfine sugar
4 medium eggs
Scant 1½ cups self-rising flour
Generous 1 cup ground almonds
1 ounce ground poppy seeds (you can grind them yourself using a mortar and pestle)
Finely grated zest of 2 lemons
For the lemon syrup
Scant ½ cup lemon juice
1 cup superfine sugar
For the glaze
1 pound 2 ounces fondant patissiere
Juice of 1 lemon
1 teaspoon glucose

equipment

10"-Kugelhupf or Bundt cake pan

Preheat the oven to 347 degrees F. Prepare the cake pan by greasing with softened butter and dusting with all-purpose flour.

To make the sponge
Place the butter, sugar, and lemon zest in a mixing bowl and cream until pale and fluffy.

Beat the eggs lightly in another bowl and slowly add to the butter mixture while whisking quickly. If the mixture starts to separate or curdle, stop adding the egg and beat in 2–3 tablespoons of the flour. This will rebind the batter. Once all the egg has been added and combined with the butter mixture, sift in the flour and add the ground almonds and poppy seeds. Stir until the batter is just combined.

Pour the batter into the prepared cake pan, using a rubber spatula to help fill the pan. Before baking, tap the filled cake pan on your work surface a few times to make sure the batter has reached all the cavities at the base of the pan.

Bake for 30 to 40 minutes, depending on your oven. The sponge is cooked when the sides are beginning to shrink away from the edges of the pan and the top is golden brown and springs back to the touch. If in doubt, insert a clean knife or wooden skewer into the center of the sponge; it should come out clean.

To make the lemon syrup
While the sponge is baking, prepare a lemon syrup for soaking. Place the lemon juice and superfine sugar into a pan and bring to a boil. Simmer until all the sugar crystals have dissolved. Set aside to cool down slightly.

Once the sponge is baked, immediately brush the sponge with half the lemon syrup; this allows the syrup to be absorbed faster.

Let cool for about 30 minutes outside of the oven. Once just warm, turn the cake out of the pan and let cool completely on a wire rack. Brush the other side of the sponge with the remaining syrup.

To make the glaze
Gently warm the fondant patissiere with the lemon juice to a thick pouring consistency. Do not to allow it to boil, as it will lose its shine. Stir in the glucose. Pour the fondant glaze over the top of the cake and let set.

Serve at room temperature.

RASPBERRY AND ROSE DOME CAKE

MADE OF THIN LAYERS OF JACONDE SPONGE FILLED WITH PURPLE RASPBERRY
AND ROSE JAM, VANILLA BUTTERCREAM, AND FRESH RASPBERRIES,
THIS IS MY PERSONAL TAKE ON THE CLASSIC SWEDISH PRINCESS CAKE.
IT IS UTTERLY DELICIOUS AND PERFECT FOR AN OCCASION.
IT IS A DELICATE CAKE, SO KEEP THE DECORATION SIMPLE.

Makes one 6"-round dome cake, serving 8 to 12 slices
To make two dome cakes, simply double the amounts given below

ingredients

For the crème patissière
2¾ ounces egg yolks
(approximately 3 small egg yolks)
½ cup + 2 tablespoons superfine sugar
1 vanilla bean
Generous 2 cups whole milk
Generous ⅓ cup cornstarch

For the Jaconde sponge
3 medium eggs
Generous 1 cup confectioners' sugar
Generous 1⅓ cups ground almonds
3 egg whites
1 tablespoon sugar
Generous ¼ cup all-purpose flour

For the filling
1⅛ cups unsalted butter, at room
temperature
1 tablespoon Eau de Vie (optional)
2 tablespoons Peggy's Purple Raspberry and
Rose Jam or any other good-quality
raspberry jam
Carton of raspberries (about 5½ ounces)

For the decoration
14 ounces marzipan
1 pound 5 ounces white rolled fondant
Brown, green, and pink paste food color
1 teaspoon gum tragacanth
Small amount of white vegetable fat
1 tablespoon apricot jam, strained
Confectioners' sugar for dusting
Small amount or clear alcohol,
such as vodka or Eau de Vie
Small amount of royal icing (see page 183)

equipment

Two cookie sheets with
a minimum width of 12"-
6"-sphere mold
(I use one half of a ball-shaped cake pan)
6"-round pastry cutter
Plastic pastry bag
6"-round thin cake card
Paper pastry bag (see page 184)
Small nonstick rolling pin
Dog rose silicone mold
(I use a mold from FPC Sugarcraft)
Primrose cutter (medium or large)
Blossom mold
(I use a mold from Blossom Sugar Art)
Egg carton or plastic paint palette with wells
Piece of ribbon, long enough to
cover the circumference of the cake
Plain round 1"-cookie cutter

1

2

3

4

5

6

7

8

9

10

11

12

13

14

15

16

This cake has a shelf life of 3 days when stored in the refrigerator, however the decoration may become soft and sticky in cold humid conditions. Therefore, I recommend making the cake no more than 2 days in advance of serving and consuming it within 1 day.

Preheat the oven to 425 degrees F.

Line two cookie sheets with baking parchment.

To make the crème patissière
Whisk the egg yolks with the superfine sugar in a mixing bowl, then add the cornstarch and stir to combine. Place the milk, vanilla seeds, and scraped vanilla bean in a pan and bring to a bare simmer. Pour about a quarter of the hot milk onto the egg yolk mixture, immediately stirring until smooth.

Return the egg yolk and milk mixture to the pan with the remaining hot milk. Continue cooking until the mixture thickens and bubbles in the center, stirring well to make sure the crème patissière does not burn on the bottom of the pan. Taste the crème patissière to check it is cooked; it should not taste floury. The texture should be smooth and thick.

Transfer to a bowl or tray. To prevent a skin from forming, cover tightly with plastic wrap, pressing down firmly to make sure there are no air pockets. Let cool and chill in the refrigerator until further use.

To make the Jaconde sponge
Beat the whole eggs and confectioners' sugar together until pale and fluffy. Sift together the flour and ground almonds, then gently fold into the egg mixture using a spatula.

In a clean dry bowl, whisk the egg whites with the sugar until they reach soft peaks. Fold the meringue mixture into the batter.

Divide the batter evenly between the two prepared cookie sheets and level the surface using a palette knife or the back of a spoon.

Bake for 8 to 10 minutes on a low shelf, depending on your oven. The sponge is cooked when the sides are beginning to shrink away from the edges of the pan and the top is lightly browned and springs back to the touch.

Let cool outside of the oven but leave the sponges on the cookie sheets. Once cool, cover with plastic wrap to prevent the sponge sheets from drying out.

To make the buttercream filling
Place the crème patissière in a bowl and beat, adding the softened butter little by little until all the butter is incorporated and the buttercream has thickened. Add the Eau de Vie.

To assemble the cake
Place the sphere mold on top of a small bowl to hold it steady. Line the inside of the mold with plastic wrap, overlapping the edges (1).

Cut out a 12"-circle from one of the sponge sheets (2–3). Use it to line the inside of the sphere mold, leaving a small overlap around the outside edge. Trim off any excess using a pair of kitchen scissors (4–7).

Fill a pastry bag with the buttercream filling. Snip 1" off the tip and pipe a thick layer into the bottom of the cake mold, then place six fresh raspberries evenly over the buttercream (8). Pipe another layer of buttercream on top (9). Continue adding layers of buttercream and fresh raspberries until you have almost reached the top edge of the mold. Level off the last layer of buttercream using a palette knife (10).

Cut out two 6"-circles from the remaining sponge sheet using a cookie cutter (11). Sandwich the two circles of sponge together with a thin layer of raspberry jam (12–13). Place the two sponge circles on top of the buttercream-filled mold (14). Spread over a thin layer of buttercream, then place the cake card on top. Trim any excess sponge from around the edges of the mold (15). Fold the overlapping plastic wrap over the top (16). Chill for at least 4 to 6 hours or preferably overnight.

To make the decoration
While your cake is setting in the refrigerator, make the flower decorations. You can make sugar flowers well in advance and store them for several months in a cool and dry place, but do not store them in an airtight container as the paste may sweat and collapse.

For the mocha-colored cake, mix 14 ounces rolled fondant with brown food color to a very pale coffee shade. For the green cake, mix 14 ounces rolled fondant with green food color to a pale pastel shade. To prevent it drying out, wrap the rolled fondant in plastic wrap.

Mix the remaining rolled fondant with a little pink food color and the gum tragacanth. Add a small amount of white vegetable fat to make the paste smooth and pliable. For the mocha cake, mix only one shade of pale pink. For the green cake, mix a few different shades of pink. Wrap the rolled fondant in plastic wrap and let rest for 30 minutes in order to firm up a little.

To make the blossoms for the mocha-colored cake, follow the instructions on page 174 using the primrose blossom cutter and mold.

To make the dog roses for the green cake, rub a thin layer of vegetable fat into the mold and press a small ball of pink rolled fondant into the embossed floral shape. Smooth and flatten the back with your fingers and, if necessary, trim off any excess paste using a small kitchen knife. To release, bend the mold outward until the flower drops out. For a similar technique, see page 174. Place the sugar flower on a curved surface, for example, inside the wells of a paint palette or an egg carton lined with waxed paper, to dry. Make 3–4 flowers in different shades of pink rolled fondant using this method.

To decorate

Once the cake has set, remove it from the refrigerator and turn it out on a sheet of waxed paper. Remove the mold and plastic wrap **(1)**. Gently warm the apricot jam and brush a thin layer all over the dome cake **(2)**.

On a surface dusted with confectioners' sugar, roll the marzipan out to a thickness 1/8 to 1/6". It must be large enough to cover the dome. Using a rolling pin, lift the rolled marzipan and lay it over the dome cake **(3)**. Smooth the marzipan down the sides of the dome using your fingers. Tuck the edges down and trim away any excess marzipan using a kitchen knife **(4)**.

Splash some clear alcohol onto your hands **(5)**. Smooth the alcohol over the marzipan-covered dome **(6)**. This creates an adhesive. Roll out the colored rolled fondant and place over the marzipan the same way **(7)**. Trim away any excess rolled fondant as before **(8)**.

For the mocha dome cake, use a piece of ribbon to determine the correct circumference of the base of the dome **(9)**. Using this ribbon as a guide for length and a ruler for depth, roll out a thin strip of the remaining pink rolled fondant **(10)**. Cut a 1"-wide strip that is long enough to go all around the base of the dome **(11)**. Using a small round cutter, cut out even half-circles from the pink rolled fondant strip to create a swag border **(12)**.

Brush the base of the dome thinly with clear alcohol **(13)**. Lay the pink rolled fondant strip all around it, with the cutout edge pointing upward **(14)**.

Mix the royal icing with brown food color to make a dark chocolate shade with a soft-peak consistency (see pages 182–3). Fill a paper pastry bag with the icing, snip a small hole from the tip of the bag, and pipe a swag border following the edge of the pink icing **(15)**. Pipe three loops at the highest points of the swags with a dot below **(16)**. Although not essential, this is best done using a turntable.

To finish, pipe small brown dots into the center of each pink blossom. Using a tiny amount of royal icing, stick a cluster of three blossoms on the top of the dome.

For the green dome cake, mix the royal icing with pink food color to make a pale shade with a soft-peak consistency (see page 182–183). Fill a paper pastry bag with the icing, snip a small hole from the tip of the bag, and pipe double swags evenly around the base of the dome and finish with a dot at all the joints.

To finish, using a tiny amount of royal icing, stick a few randomly placed dog roses on top of the dome.

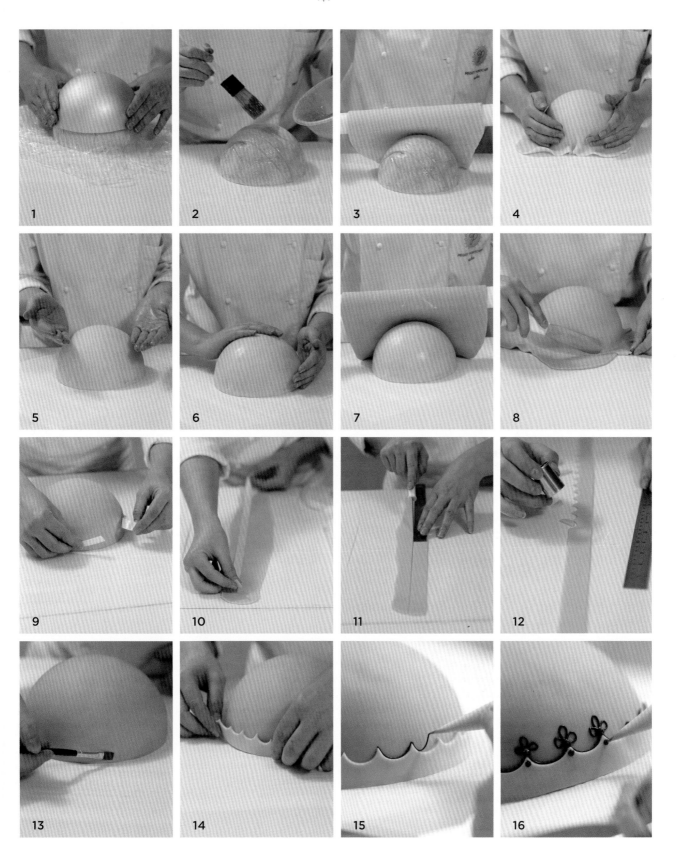

MINI EGGNOG KUGELHOPFS

BASED ON A TRADITIONAL BAVARIAN RECIPE, THESE LITTLE CAKES
ARE PERFECT WITH AN AFTERNOON CUP OF COFFEE.
THE WORD "KUGEL" MEANS DOME IN GERMAN, REFLECTING THE
CLASSIC SHAPE PAN THESE CAKES ARE BAKED IN.
Makes 12 individual kugelhopfs

ingredients

Small amount of unsalted butter, softened for
greasing the cake molds
6 medium eggs
Scant 2⅓ cups confectioners' sugar, sifted
Seeds of 1 vanilla bean
1¼ cups vegetable oil
1¼ cups Advocaat
Generous 1 cup all-purpose flour, sifted plus
extra for dusting
Generous 1 cup cornstarch, sifted
2 heaping teaspoons baking powder
Pinch of salt
Scant ¾ cup Advocaat, plus extra for
serving (optional)
Scant ¾ cup rum
Confectioners' sugar for dusting

equipment

Two mini Kugelhopf trays, each with 6 molds
approximately 4" in diameter

Preheat the oven to 400 degrees F. Prepare the cake molds by greasing with softened butter and dusting with all-purpose flour.

Place the eggs, confectioners' sugar, and vanilla seeds in the bowl of an electric mixer and whisk together until pale and fluffy. Add the vegetable oil and the eggnog and mix until just combined.

Sift the flour, cornstarch, and baking powder together and fold it through the egg mixture.

Divide the batter evenly between the Kugelhopf trays, filling each mold until two-thirds full only. If you find it difficult to measure by eye, use your kitchen scales to weigh out the amount of cake batter for each mold.

Place the tray in the oven and turn the temperature down to 350 degrees F. Bake for 15 minutes, then turn the tray around and bake for another 10 to 15 minutes. The cakes are cooked when the sides are beginning to shrink away from the edges of the molds and the tops are golden brown and spring back to the touch. If in doubt, insert a clean knife or wooden skewer into the center of each cake; it should come out clean. Once the cakes are baked, let them rest for a few minutes outside of the oven before turning them out of the molds.

Combine the rum and Advocaat, then using a pastry brush, soak the tops of the cakes with the alcohol while they are still warm. Let cool completely on a wire rack.

Serve at room temperature. Dust the tops of the cakes with confectioners' sugar before serving. If preferred, serve with a drop of extra Advocaat.

CHOCOLATE BATTENBERG CAKE

A CONTEMPORARY TWIST ON A TRADITIONAL DESIGN, THE DARK AND LIGHT SQUARES REMIND ME OF SMALL CHECKERBOARDS AND THIS CAKE WOULD BE GREAT FOR A QUEEN OF HEARTS TEA PARTY. IT TASTES DELICIOUS, TOO!

Makes 3 rectangular cakes of approximately 8" long, serving 8 slices each

ingredients

1⅛ cups unsalted butter, softened
1¼ cups superfine sugar
Seeds of 1 vanilla bean
Generous 1⅔ cups self-rising flour
Generous 1 cup ground almonds
½ cup unsweetened cocoa powder
6 medium eggs
1 heaping tablespoon apricot jam, strained
1 pound 10 ounces marzipan
Brown paste food color
Confectioners' sugar, for dusting

equipment

Two 8"-square cake pans
Pair of cake smoothers
Marzipan crimper

Bake the sponges one day ahead of assembling and serving.

Preheat the oven to 350 degrees F. Prepare the cake pans by lining them with waxed paper. For full instructions on how to do this, see page 87.

To make the sponge
Place the butter, superfine sugar, and vanilla seeds in a mixing bowl and cream together until pale and fluffy.

Beat the eggs lightly in a pitcher and slowly pour into the butter mixture while mixing on high speed to incorporate.

Divide the batter into two equal parts. Sift 1 cup flour and ½ cup almonds together and fold through the first half of the batter. Then sift generous ⅔ cup flour, ½ cup almonds, and the cocoa powder together and fold through the second half. Pour each batter into a prepared cake pan.

Bake for 25–30 minutes, depending on your oven. The sponges are cooked when the sides are beginning to shrink away from the edges of the pan and tops spring back to the touch. If in doubt, insert a clean knife or wooden skewer into the center; it should come out clean.

Let cool for about 30 minutes outside of the oven. Once just warm, turn the cakes out of the pans and let cool completely on a wire rack. Once cool, wrap the sponges in plastic wrap and then rest them overnight at room temperature. This will ensure that the sponges firm up to the perfect texture for trimming and layering. When trimmed too soon after baking, the sponges tend to crumble and may even break into pieces.

To assemble the cake
Level the tops of the sponges using a serrated knife to an overall height of 1". Trim off the edges and cut each sponge into three even strips of about 2" wide so you have three white and three brown sponge pieces all of the same size. For each Battenberg cake you need one brown and one white piece of sponge.

Gently warm the apricot jam and spread a thin layer over one of the dark sponges (1). Place one of the light sponges on top, then cut them in half lengthwise and lay flat (2). Brush another thin layer of jam over the surface of one half slice and then place the second half slice on top, with the colors facing the opposite way to create a grid of four squares when viewed from the front. Repeat for the other pieces of sponge or, alternatively, freeze them for later use.

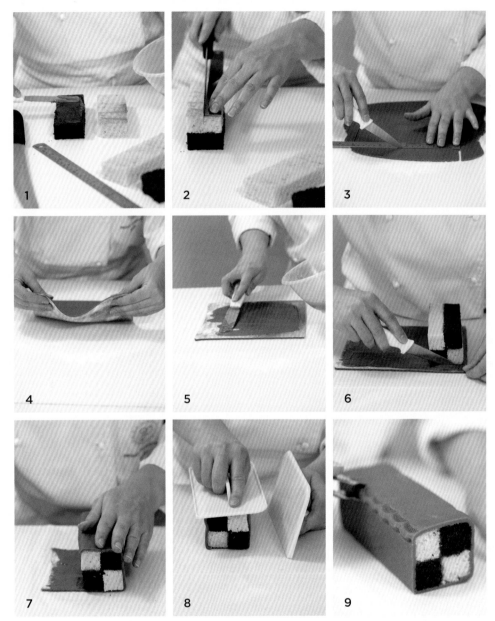

THE CHECKERBOARD EFFECT OF THE CAKE IS CREATED BY LAYERING TWO COLORS OF SPONGE. THE SIMPLE MARZIPAN COVERING IS GIVEN ADDED VISUAL INTEREST USING CRIMPERS.

Mix the marzipan with the brown food color to a light shade. On a surface dusted with confectioners' sugar, roll the marzipan out to a thickness of ⅛ to ⅙". It must be large enough that you can cut a 8" square. Using a ruler and kitchen knife, cut out a 8" square **(3)**. Flip it over onto a clean surface or sheet of waxed paper **(4)**. Spread a thin layer of jam over the marzipan sheet **(5)**. Place the sponge log on top of the marzipan toward one side. If necessary, trim the marzipan sheet to the same length as the log **(6)**. Making sure the ends meet at one of the corners, carefully wrap the marzipan around the log **(7)**. Trim away any excess. Press the join together with your fingers.

Square up the sides by gently pressing them with the cake smoothers **(8)**. For extra detail, crimp along the top corners using a marzipan crimper **(9)**.

TRIPLE BERRY CHEESECAKES

THESE STUNNING LITTLE CHEESECAKES ARE VERY EASY TO MAKE AND TASTE FABULOUS. THEY HAVE A VERY LIGHT TEXTURE AND CONSIST OF LAYERS OF STRAWBERRY, RASPBERRY, AND BLUEBERRY.

Makes 16 individual cheesecakes

ingredients

For the cookie base
7 tablespoons melted butter
2 tablespoons runny honey
7 ounces Graham crackers, finely crushed
1 teaspoon ground cinnamon
For the cheesecake
6 gelatin leaves
Scant ½ cup blueberry puree
Scant ½ cup raspberry puree
Scant ½ cup strawberry puree
(if you can't find berry purees, make your own by pureeing fresh berries in a blender and passing them through a fine strainer)
2¾ cups regular cream cheese
Scant 1 cup superfine sugar
Scant 1 cup crème fraîche
Scant 3 cups heavy or whipping cream

equipment

Sixteen 2"-round dessert rings or mousse molds
2"-deep acetate strips
Three plastic pastry bags

Line the insides of the dessert rings or mousse molds with the acetate strips.

To make the cookie base
Melt the butter with the honey in a pan. Add the crushed cookies and cinnamon and mix until combined. Carefully press a tablespoonful of the cookie mixture into the bottom of each mold, keeping the sides as clean as possible.

To make the cheesecake
Place the gelatin leaves into a bowl and soak them in cold water. Gently warm each of the fruit purees separately, squeeze the water from the gelatin leaves and dissolve two leaves in each of the hot fruit purees. Let cool.

Place the cream cheese and superfine sugar in a bowl and mix together until smooth and combined. Then add the crème fraîche. Whip the cream to a soft-peak consistency, taking care not to overwhip.

Divide the cream cheese mixture into three equal parts. Once the fruit purees have cooled to room temperature, mix each one separately with a third of the cream cheese mixture, using a whisk. From this point, you must work quickly as the gelatin can set.

Divide the whipped cream into three equal parts. Gently fold through each of the three cream cheese mixtures until combined.

Starting with strawberry, followed by raspberry and then blueberry, layer the three fruit mixtures in the lined rings or molds. I find it easier and neater to use pastry bags to create the different layers. However, if you do not have pastry bags you can carefully spoon the mixtures into the molds instead.

If using pastry bags, fill a plastic pastry bag with each mixture. Snip 1" from the tip of the bag and pipe a layer over the bottom of the cookie base to about halfway up the sides. Repeat for the two other fruit mixtures until you reach the top.

Flatten the top layers with a palette knife or the back of a spoon. Chill for at least 4 hours or until set.

You can make these cheesecakes up to 3 days in advance if stored in the refrigerator. Demold and remove the acetate strips just before serving.

BANANA LOAF CAKE WITH BANANA FROSTING

FOR MAXIMUM FLAVOR USE OVERRIPE BANANAS AND ENJOY THE CAKE ONE DAY
AFTER BAKING SO THE FLAVORS HAVE TIME TO MATURE.

Makes 1 large loaf cake, serving 8 to 12 slices

ingredients

7 tablespoons butter, softened plus extra for
greasing
1 cup light brown sugar
1 teaspoon ground cinnamon
2 medium eggs
10½ ounces overripe bananas
Generous 1¼ cups all-purpose flour
1 teaspoon baking soda
2½ ounces semisweet chocolate (minimum
53% cocoa solids), chopped or in buttons
Generous ¾ cup walnuts, toasted and roughly
chopped

For the banana frosting
See page 56

equipment

Large 9"- by 5"-loaf pan

Preheat the oven to 347 degrees F.

Prepare the loaf pan by greasing it with butter.

To make the cake
Place the butter, light brown sugar, and
ground cinnamon in a mixing bowl and cream
together until pale and fluffy.

Beat the eggs lightly and slowly add to the
butter mixture while mixing on high speed to
incorporate.

Mash up the bananas and add to the batter,
followed by the chocolate and walnuts.

Sift the flour and baking soda together and
add to the batter on low speed until just
combined. Pour the batter into the prepared
cake pan.

Bake for 35–40 minutes, depending on your
oven. The cake is cooked when the top springs
back to the touch. If in doubt, insert a clean
knife or wooden skewer into the center of the
cake; it should come out clean.

Let cool for a few minutes outside of the oven
before turning the cake out of the pan. Let
cool completely on a wire rack.

To make the frosting
Following the directions on page 58, make the
banana frosting.

Once cool, spread the top of the cake with the
frosting using a palette knife. Chill for about 30
minutes to set the frosting.

Serve at room temperature.

LIGHT LUXURY FRUIT CAKE

LIGHT AND MOIST WITH FRUITY FLAVORS, THIS CAKE HAS AN ADDITIONAL
CRUNCH FROM THE DRIED FIGS. TO CREATE A CONTEMPORARY CHRISTMAS CAKE
WITH A SENSE OF OPULENCE, I TOOK INSPIRATION FROM THE WORLD OF
INTERIOR DESIGN AND USED DAMASK STENCILS, OVALS, AND STAGS WITH GOLD LUSTER.
USING STENCILS WITH ROYAL ICING LOOKS SCARIER THAN IT IS, I SUGGEST
TESTING IT ON A PIECE OF PAPER FIRST TO GET A FEELING FOR THE
TECHNIQUE BEFORE DECORATING THE CAKE.

Makes one 6"- by 8"-oval cake, serving 20 finger slices

ingredients

For the fruit mix
Scant 1 cup raisins
Generous ⅓ cup dried cranberries, halved
1⅓ cups golden raisins, roughly chopped
4½ ounces whole candied cherries
3 ounces dried figs, chopped
1 ounce sour cherries, chopped
¼ cup whisky
Scant ¼ cup dark corn syrup
Grated zest of 1 lemon

For the cake mix
4½ ounces eggs (approximately
2 small eggs)
½ cup dark brown sugar
8 tablespoons unsalted butter, softened
Generous ¼ cup ground almonds
Scant ⅔ cup all-purpose flour
¼ teaspoon ground cinnamon
Pinch of ground cloves
Pinch of ground nutmeg
Pinch of salt
2 tablespoons whisky for soaking

For the decoration
1 tablespoon apricot jam, strained
1 pound 5 ounces marzipan
1 pound 12 ounces ivory rolled fondant
9 ounces white florists paste
Small amount of white vegetable fat
Ivory and brown food paste color
Small amount of edible gold luster
Small amount of unsweetened cocoa powder
(for the brown stag only)
About 5½ ounces royal icing
Small amount of clear alcohol,
such as vodka or Eau de Vie
Small amount of piping gel
Confectioners' sugar, for dusting

equipment

6"- by 8"-oval cake card
8"- by 10"-oval cake board
Approximately 5ft of ¼"-wide satin
ribbon to cover the base of the cake and board
Small piece of double-sided sticky tape
6"- by 8"-oval cake pan
Newspaper and string for insulating cake pan
Pair of marzipan spacers
Pair of cake smoothers
Paper pastry bag
Laser-cut damask cake stencil
Oval cutter of about 5" by 3"
Silicon stag mold (I use a mould
from First Impressions)
Large soft powder brush
Fine artist's brush

Make this cake at least 3–4 days in advance and store it wrapped in a layer of waxed paper, then in aluminum foil, to preserve moisture and flavor. You can make it several weeks, if not months, in advance if stored in a cool dry place. For an extra-moist and boozy flavor, feed the cake with whisky on a weekly basis or several times before icing.

To make the fruit mix
Place all the ingredients for the fruit mix into a large bowl, stir well and cover with plastic wrap. Let infuse overnight at room temperature.

Preheat the oven to 275 degrees F. Double-line a deep 6"-round or oval cake pan with waxed paper and wrap the pan with a double thickness of brown paper, securing it with string.

To make the cake mix
Place the eggs and sugar in a medium bowl and whisk by hand until combined.

In a separate bowl, cream together the butter and the ground almonds until just creamy but not too aerated. Slowly add the egg mixture until you have a smooth emulsion. If the mixture starts to separate or curdle, add 1 tablespoon of flour. This will rebind the batter.

Sift the remaining dry ingredients together and fold through the batter in two batches until just combined.

Add the infused fruit to the cake batter and combine thoroughly and evenly with either a spatula or clean, gloved hands.

Pour the cake batter into the prepared pan. Level the surface with the back of a spoon. Before baking, tap the filled cake pan on the surface a few times to release any large air bubbles. This prevents the surface of the cake cracking.

Bake on a low shelf for 2 to 3 hours, depending on your oven. To prevent the cake from over-browning, place an empty tray on the rack above. The cake is cooked when the top is golden brown. If in doubt, insert a clean knife or wooden skewer into the center of the cake: it should come out clean.

Let cool for 10 minutes outside of the oven. While still warm, brush the top of the cake with whisky. Le the cake cool completely on a wire rack before wrapping in waxed paper and aluminum foil.

To decorate the cake and board
Unwrap the cake and place it upside down on the smaller cake board. Gently warm the apricot jam and use it to adhere the cake to the board. If there are any gaps between the cake and the board, fill them with small pieces of marzipan. Place the cake and board on a sheet of waxed paper. Brush a thin layer of warmed apricot jam over the top and sides of the cake.

On a surface dusted with confectioners' sugar, roll the marzipan out to a thickness of ¼" using spacers. It must be large enough to cover the cake. Using a rolling pin, lift the rolled marzipan and lay it over the cake. Smooth the marzipan over the cake, flattening the top and sides, using your hands. Trim away any excess marzipan using a kitchen knife. Flatten the top and sides of the cake using cake smoothers until even.

Brush some clear alcohol over the marzipan-covered cake to create an adhesive. Roll out the ivory rolled fondant and place over the marzipan in the same way. Trim away any excess as before, reserving the trimmings for covering the cake board. Let set overnight.

Meanwhile, brush some clear alcohol over the larger cake board. Roll the remaining ivory rolled fondant out to a thickness of 1/8" and lay over the board. Press down with one of the cake smoothers and trim away any excess leaving a small overlap all around the edges, reserving the trimmings for making the plaque.

Pick up the covered board with one hand and, using your other, push the overlapping rolled

fondant down with the smoother until it falls off, creating a clean chamfered edge. Use a kitchen knife with a plain edge to cut off any remaining rolled fondant from the sides of the board. Let set overnight.

The following day, spread a thin layer of royal icing on the center of the covered board and place the cake on top. Make sure no icing shows from under the edge. Let set for at least 30 minutes.

To decorate the sides of the cake

To recreate the design of the larger cake you need two paper pastry bags (see page 184) filled with royal icing at soft-peak consistency (see page 183), one colored brown and the other colored ivory. To recreate the design of the smaller cake you need ivory royal icing only.

For the damask design, mix the remaining royal icing with brown soft-peak icing (1–3).

For the swag design, mix it with ivory. Hold the stencil tight and flat on the side of the cake (4). If possible, get someone to assist by holding the stencil in place while you spread the icing over the top (5). Once the design is covered (6), carefully remove the stencil (7). Make sure you do not get any icing on the clean rolled fondant. Let dry. Clean the stencil each time before applying the next pattern onto the cake.

For the brown damask design, outline the details with the ivory soft-peak icing (8).

For the ivory swag design, outlines are not required. Once dry, mix the gold luster with a drop of alcohol and piping gel to create a thick golden paint (9). Use it to paint either the outlines of the damask pattern or the ivory swag detail, using a fine artist's brush (10).

To make the oval plaque

Mix 2¾ ounces rolled fondant with 2¾ ounces flower paste. If sticky, knead in a small amount of vegetable fat. For the large cake, color the paste with ivory food color. For the small cake, color the paste with brown food color.

On a surface lightly dusted with confectioners' sugar, roll the paste out to a thickness of ⅟₁₆". Using an oval cutter, cut out an oval and place it on top of a sheet of waxed paper. For the larger cake, generously dust the ivory oval plaque with gold luster. Make sure that the sides are covered as well as the top.

Brush the middle of the cake with a thin layer of clear alcohol. Lay the plaque centered on top.

To make the stag

For the brown stag, mix the remaining flower paste with a small amount of white vegetable fat and brown food color. For the golden stag, mix the flower paste with ivory food color. For the brown stag, brush the inside of the stag mold generously with cocoa. For the golden stag, brush with gold luster (11). Make sure all gaps and corners of the mold are covered.

Press the florist's paste inside the mold; use individual pieces for the smaller more delicate areas (12). Rub the back surface of the stag until smooth and to ensure all the pieces of its body are holding together. Trim away any excess paste until the back of the stag is perfectly level (13–14).

To release the stag, bend the mold from the inside out until the stag falls out (15). Let dry for a short time. Once the stag feels slightly set, carefully transfer it onto the plaque and stick it down with edible glue.

To pipe a frame around the plaque

Using the pastry bag filled with the soft peak icing, pipe a simple C-scroll border around the edge of the plaque. Pipe small teardrops and dots between each scroll to create a pretty design to frame the plaque. To get a feel for the scale and continuity of the piped design, practice the border on a piece of paper first before piping directly onto the cake (16).

If using the ivory icing, paint the border with gold luster once dry. Finish the cake with either a satin ribbon or a row of piped dots around the base.

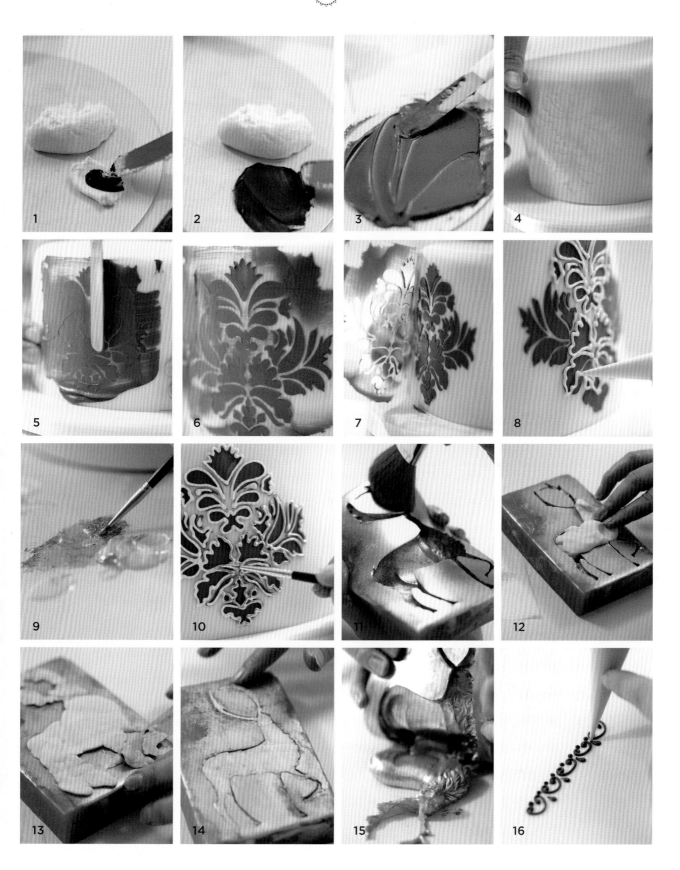

DELICIOUS DRINKS

PINK LEMONADE

OUR PINK LEMONADE IS A FAVORITE AT THE PARLOUR AND GOES
HAND-IN-HAND WITH A YUMMY CUPCAKE. THE CRANBERRY JUICE PROVIDES THE
PRETTY PINK COLOR. FOR OTHER VARIATIONS, ADD BLACK CURRANT JUICE
FOR A DEEPER CERISE PINK OR KIWI JUICE FOR A LIGHT GREEN.

Makes approximately 4 glasses

ingredients

Scant ½ cup freshly squeezed lemon juice
½ cup superfine sugar
Generous 2 cups water
¼ cup cranberry or raspberry juice
Ice cubes and lemon slices, to serve

equipment

Juicer or citrus press
Pan
Glass pitcher or teapot
Tall glasses

Place the lemon juice, superfine sugar, and
water in a pan and bring to a boil. Simmer until
the sugar crystals have dissolved, then set aside
to cool.

Once cool, add the cranberry juice.

Serve cold in tall glasses with lots of ice and
slices of fresh lemon.

MINTEANI

A LIGHT AND REFRESHING ICED MINT TEA COCKTAIL
PERFECT FOR A SUMMER PARTY. SERVE IN STYLISH VINTAGE TEACUPS
TO CREATE A SOPHISTICATED YET RELAXED LOOK.
Makes approximately 4 teacups

ingredients

Handful of fresh mint leaves
1 teaspoon Peggy's Peppermint & Green Tea Leaves
or any other good-quality peppermint tea
⅔ cup water
2/3 cup freshly squeezed lemon juice
¾ cup superfine sugar
¼ cup vodka
A splash of Crème de Menthe
A splash of freshly squeezed lime juice
Ice cubes

equipment

Juicer or citrus press
Pan
Glass pitcher or teapot
(with an infuser, if using loose-leaf tea)
Vintage teacups

Pick the fine leaf tips off the fresh mint twigs and place into iced water to keep them fresh.

Place the remaining mint leaves together with the peppermint tea into a glass pitcher or teapot.

Bring the water to a boil and pour over the peppermint and green tea leaves. Let infuse for 3 minutes. Let cool.

Place the lemon juice and superfine sugar in a pan and bring to a boil. Simmer until the sugar crystals have dissolved, then let cool.

Once the liquids are cool, mix them together and add the vodka, Crème de Menthe, and lime juice. Chill.

Serve cold in vintage teacups with ice and the fine leaf tips of fresh mint.

SUMMER BERRY ICE TEA

THIS IS A REFRESHING DRINK, PERFECT FOR A HOT SUMMER'S DAY.

Makes approximately 4 glasses

ingredients

1¾ cups water

4 teaspoons Peggy's Summer Berry Tea Leaves or any other
good-quality mixed berry tea

Juice of 1 lemon

Juice of 1 orange

¼ cup superfine sugar

Ice cubes and fresh mixed summer berries, to serve

equipment

Juicer or citrus press

Glass pitcher or teapot (with infuser, if using loose-leaf tea)

Short glasses

Place the summer berry tea leaves into a glass
pitcher or teapot.

Bring the water to a boil and pour over the
summer berry tea leaves. Let infuse for 3 to 5
minutes. Let cool.

Place the lemon, orange juice, and superfine
sugar in a pan and bring to a boil. Simmer until
the sugar crystals have dissolved, then set aside
to cool.

Once the liquids are cool, mix them together.
Chill.

Serve cold in short glasses with ice and a few
fresh summer berries.

HOT WHITE CHOCOLATE
WITH VANILLA

A WONDERFUL WINTER WARMER FOR THE SERIOUSLY SWEET-TOOTHED.
SERVE WITH SPICED CHRISTMAS COOKIES OR JUST ENJOY ON ITS OWN.

Makes approximately 4 glasses

ingredients

⅔ cup whipping cream
1¼ cups milk
Pinch ground nutmeg
Seeds of ½ vanilla bean
5½ ounces white chocolate

equipment

Pan
Tall glass mugs

Place the cream, milk, nutmeg, and vanilla seeds
(you can also add the bean but remove it before
adding the cream to the chocolate) in a pan and
bring to a bare simmer.

Place the chocolate in a mixing bowl and pour
over the hot cream. Whisk together until the
chocolate has melted.

Serve warm in tall glass mugs.

HOMEMADE HOT CHOCOLATE

A CHOCOHOLIC'S DELIGHT! USING REAL CHOCOLATE INSTEAD OF JUST COCOA POWDER MAKES ALL THE DIFFERENCE. THIS IS A SUMPTUOUS RECIPE THAT WILL GIVE YOU AN INSTANT HIT OF HAPPINESS.

Makes approximately 2 mugs or 3 to 4 teacups

ingredients

4½ ounces semisweet chocolate (minimum 53% cocoa solids), chopped or in buttons
2 teaspoons unsweetened cocoa powder, plus extra for dusting (optional)
½ cup whipping cream
1¼ cups milk
Seeds of ½ vanilla bean

equipment

Pan
Teacups
Stencil (optional)

Place the cream, milk, and vanilla seeds (you can also add the bean but remove it before adding the cream to the chocolate) in a pan and bring to a bare simmer.

Place the chocolate in a mixing bowl and sift in the cocoa powder. Pour over the hot cream. Whisk together until the chocolate has melted.

Return to the pan and heat again for a few more minutes while stirring. Do not allow to boil as the chocolate can burn and become bitter. Taste to make sure the cocoa powder has completely dissolved. Pass through a strainer.

Serve warm in teacups.

For a pretty patterned effect, place a small stencil over the rim of the teacup and dust with cocoa powder.

BANANA & PEANUT BUTTER SMOOTHIE

THIS DELICIOUS ENERGIZING DRINK IS ENJOYED BY YOUNG AND OLD
AND GREAT FOR USING UP OVERRIPE BANANAS.
I LOVE DRINKING IT IN THE MORNING AS IT MAKES A QUICK
AND WHOLESOME BREAKFAST.

Makes about 2 glasses

ingredients

2 very ripe bananas
1½ cups cold milk
1 tablespoons smooth peanut butter
1–2 teaspoons honey (depending on the ripeness of
the bananas)

equipment

Freestanding or hand blender with a pitcher
Tall glasses
Straws

Place all the ingredients into the pitcher and
blend until smooth and frothy.

Serve immediately in tall glasses.

MULLED WINE

MULLED WINE IS ONE OF MY FAVORITE CHRISTMAS TREATS AND REMINDS ME OF THE WONDERFUL HOURS I HAVE SPENT AT GERMAN CHRISTMAS MARKETS NEAR MY HOME, STANDING KNEE-DEEP IN SNOW. MULLED WINE, OR GLÜHWEIN AS I CALL IT, TASTES DELICIOUS WITH TRADITIONAL CHRISTMAS COOKIES SUCH AS MY MULLED WINE COOKIES (SEE PAGES 52–3) OR GINGERBREAD (SEE PAGES 50–51). FOR A FESTIVE TOUCH, I SERVE THE MULLED WINE IN UNIQUE VINTAGE TEACUP WINE GLASSES.

Makes about 4 teacups

ingredients

1 orange, plus extra slices for serving
Generous 2 cups red wine
Scant ¼ cup green ginger wine
Scant ½ cup water
Generous ⅛ cup superfine sugar
1 teaspoon cloves, crushed
2 cinnamon sticks, crushed, plus extra
for serving
½ teaspoon ground nutmeg
1 star anise, crushed, plus extra for serving

equipment

Potato peeler
Pan
Fine strainer or cheesecloth
Vintage teacup wine glasses or any other
beautiful heatproof glasses or mugs

Peel the rind from the orange and cut it in half.

Place the orange peel, orange halves, and all the other ingredients in a pan. Gently warm for about 20 minutes. Do not allow it to boil.

Take the pan off the heat, cover the top with plastic wrap or a lid, and let infuse for at least 30 minutes.

Once infused, strain through a fine strainer to remove the peel and spices.

Serve warm in vintage teacup wine glasses.

THE ICING
ON THE CAKE

In this chapter I demonstrate the decorating techniques and other finishing touches used to assemble and embellish the cakes and confections throughout this book. It's called The Icing on the Cake because all the techniques and recipes given here will add that touch of finesse to your baking. This chapter is a helpful resource of easy-to-follow tips on making simple sugar blossoms, frosting, icing cakes and cupcakes, and making royal icing for piped decorations. As the quantities vary with each recipe, here are some basic ratios and explanations for the most essential ingredients used:

Soft modeling rolled fondant On its own rolled fondant is too soft for molding and tears during the process so I mix it with gum tragacanth, which is a tasteless, water-soluble natural gum used as a hardening or thickening agent. The ratio is roughly 1 teaspoon gum tragacanth to 10½ ounces rolled fondant, depending on the required stiffness. It does tend to make the rolled fondant a little dry, so add a dab of white vegetable fat to make the paste smooth and pliable again. Once mixed, the rolled fondant needs to rest for about 30 minutes to firm up. As the paste dries out quickly when exposed to air it should be covered with plastic wrap or placed in a plastic bag.

Edible glue You can by ready-made edible glue, but I tend to make mine by mixing 1 teaspoon gum tragacanth with ⅔ cup water. You can also use CMC instead of gum tragacanth. At first the mixture will be lumpy but, when stirred occasionally, the powder will slowly swell and combine with the water to make a smooth and thick gel. If it stiffens too much, just add a little more water. The consistency should be a bit softer than hair gel. I use edible glue to stick together rolled fondant or flower paste.

Royal icing You can buy ready-made royal confectioners' sugar, which is confectioners' sugar premixed with powdered egg white, and all you have to do is add water. These mixes work very well but can be a little costly. I make my royal icing from sifted cane confectioners' sugar as it is finer than beet confectioners' sugar. The ratio of confectioners' sugar to liquid egg white (be it fresh, pasteurized, or powdered mixed with water) is 6:1. So for 15 cups confectioners' sugar you need generous 2 cups liquid. This is a good guide for a general recipe that you can scale up or down as required. When making royal icing, it is crucial that all your equipment is grease-free as otherwise the icing will not propertly stiffen. Likewise take great care not to get any yolk in with your white when separating your eggs.

basic baking kit

Freestanding electric mixer with whisk
and paddle attachment, for example
from KitchenAid or Kenwood
Food processor or hand blender
A set of different sized mixing bowls
Measuring cup or pitcher
Rubber spatula
Pastry brush with natural or synthetic bristles
(silicone brushes do not pick up enough liquid)
Selection of cookie sheets
Large nonstick rolling pin
Pair of marzipan spacers
Fine strainer for dusting and sifting flour and
confectioners' sugar
Small and large palette knife
Sharp pair of scissors
Cake leveler or long serrated kitchen knife
Small plain edged kitchen knife
Wire rack
Deep pan
Metal disk or other flat disk
(such as the loose base of a springform cake
pan)
Nonslip tilting turntable
Plastic pastry bags
Plastic wrap
Silicone or waxed paper

SIMPLE DAISIES & LEAVES

you will need

White rolled fondant
White vegetable fat
Yellow and green paste food color
Petal dust (optional)
Small amount of royal icing mixed to soft-peak consistency and colored to a pale yellow shade (see page 183)

equipment

Small nonstick plastic board with nonslip mat
Small nonstick plastic rolling pin
Daisy plunge cutter, or similar
Small leaf cutter
Dresden or veining tool
Perforated foam pad
Plastic artist's palette with 10 wells, or use perforated foam pad
Fine artist's brush (optional)
Paper pastry bag (see page 184)

To make a daisy Knead the rolled fondant with a small amount of white vegetable fat until smooth and pliable. Roll out the paste to a thickness of approximately 1/16".

Place the daisy cutter on the paste and press firmly. Lift off the cutter and, using your fingers, clean up the petal edges. Release the daisy from the cutter on to the foam pad. Using the veining tool, score down the center of each petal. Place the daisy in a well of the palette or on the foam pad and let set.

To add a yellow center to the daisy, use a paper pastry bag filled with pale yellow royal icing in a soft-peak consistency. Pipe a small dot in the center of the flower. Let dry.

To make a leaf Knead the rolled fondant with a small amount of green paste food color and then white vegetable fat until smooth and pliable. Roll out the green paste to a thickness of approximately 1/16".

Place the small leaf cutter firmly on the green paste and press. Lift off the cutter and release the leaf from the cutter on to the foam pad. Using the veining tool, score down the center of the leaf to create a curved shape. Leave on the foam pad to set.

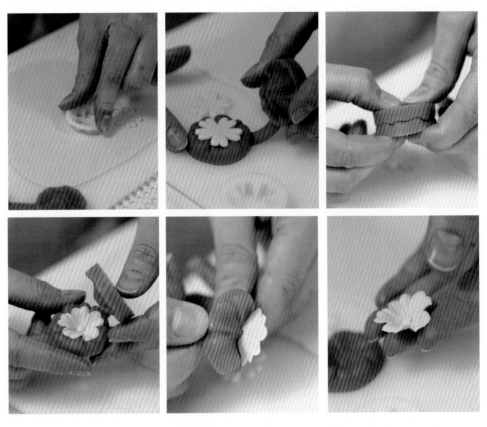

QUICK & EASY BLOSSOMS

you will need

White rolled fondant colored with paste food color, as required
White vegetable fat
Petal dust (optional)
Small amount of royal icing mixed to a soft-peak consistency (see page 183)

equipment

Small nonstick plastic board with nonslip mat
Small nonstick plastic rolling pin
Blossom cutter
Blossom veiner
Plastic artist's palette with 10 wells, or use perforated foam pad
Fine artist's brush (optional)
Paper pastry bag (optional)

Knead the rolled fondant with a small amount of paste food color, if using, and then white vegetable fat until smooth and pliable. Roll out the paste to a thickness of approximately $\frac{1}{16}$".

Place the blossom cutter on the paste and press firmly. Lift off the cutter and release the blossom. Cut a few at a time. Lightly grease the blossom veiner with white vegetable fat. One by one, place each blossom shape in the veiner and press. Carefully bend the veiner outward to release the shaped blossom and place in a well of a palette or on a foam pad. Let set for at least a few hours or preferably overnight.

Once dry, you can add shades of color to your blossoms by brushing with a tiny amount of petal dust using a fine artist's brush. If required, pipe a small dot of icing in the center of the blossom and let dry.

CHRYSANTHEMUMS

you will need

White rolled fondant colored with paste food color, as required
Gum tragacanth
White vegetable fat
Chrysanthemum silicone mold (I use one from First Impressions)

Knead the rolled fondant with small amounts of gum tragacanth until firm and pliable. Add the food color to achieve the required shade. If the paste feels sticky, add a small amount of white vegetable fat. Wrap the paste in plastic wrap and leave for 15 to 30 minutes to firm up. Rub a thin layer of white vegetable fat over the mold. Press a walnut-size piece of paste firmly into the mold. Smooth the surface with a palette knife and clean up the edges with your fingers. Carefully bend the mold outward to release the flower.

RICE-PAPER BLOSSOMS

you will need

Sheets of edible rice paper
Edible pearl luster spray in pink, blue, and green
Flower paper punch

Spray the rice paper with the edible pearl luster and let dry for a few minutes. Keep the rice paper as flat as possible as the spray will make it curl slightly.

Using the paper punch, cut out the flower shapes.

APPLIQUÉ BLOSSOMS

you will need

White rolled fondant colored with paste food color, a required
Gum tragacanth
White vegetable fat
A small amount of clear alcohol, such as vodka, or edible glue (see page 172)

equipment

Small nonstick plastic board with nonslip mat
Small nonstick plastic rolling pin
Selection of blossom cutters in different shapes and sizes
Fine artist's brush

Knead the rolled fondant with small amounts of gum tragacanth until firm and pliable. Add the food color to achieve the required shade then knead in a small amount of vegetable fat until smooth and pliable. Roll out the paste to a thickness of approximately ¹⁄₁₆". When not in use, wrap the paste in plastic wrap to prevent it drying out. Place a blossom cutter on the paste and press firmly. Lift off the cutter and release the blossom. Cut as many different shapes, sizes, and colors as required. Brush a small amount of clear alcohol or edible glue onto a large blossom and place a medium-sized blossom on top. Layer as many different sizes and colors together as required. Let set slightly before applying to the cake.

tip

The appliqué blossoms should be set enough that they hold their shape, but pliable enough that you can place them on curved surfaces without the paste cracking.

FALL LEAVES

you will need

Marzipan
White vegetable fat
Edible copper and gold luster powder

equipment

Fall leaf silicone mold
(I use one from First Impressions)
Small nonstick plastic rolling pin
Large soft powder brush
Perforated foam pad to dry leaves

Make the leaves at least one day ahead of use to allow them enough time to set. Knead the marzipan until smooth and pliable. Rub a thin layer of white vegetable fat over the mold. Place a walnut-size piece of marzipan into the mold and, using a rolling pin, press down until the marzipan covers the leaf design. Flatten and smooth the surface with your fingers until it is an even thickness, then trim away any excess marzipan with a kitchen knife.

Carefully bend the mold outward to release the leaf. Place the leaf on a small piece of waxed paper. For an fall effect, brush the leaf with a mixture of edible copper and gold luster powder. Transfer the leaf to a foam flower pad and let set.

tip

I use marzipan rather than rolled fondant for these leaves as its natural oil enhances the metallic luster. If too soft, knead in a little confectioners' sugar or gum tragacanth into the marzipan until firm.

FROSTING CUPCAKES
USING A PASTRY BAG AND ROUND TIP

Whether you are using a plain round tip or a star tip, the technique for piping frosting onto cupcakes is the same.

To prepare the plastic pastry bag, snip the end to make an opening large enough for the tip. Fit the tip then fill the pastry bag with frosting that is soft but still cool enough to hold its shape when piped. Twist the open end of the bag closed and hold it in a fist to prevent the frosting from oozing out the top.

Hold the pastry bag vertically with the tip close to the center of the cupcake. Squeeze the bag until the frosting comes out: the pressure should be coming from your fist. Hold the tip of the pastry bag steady with your free hand.

As the frosting spreads, move the tip from the center of the cupcake to around the outside while squeezing at a steady pressure.

When you have gone once around the outside of the cupcake, slowly come back to the center. Pipe another layer over the first one.

Once you reach the center of the cupcake, stop squeezing, then lightly push the tip down into the frosting just a few inches and lift the tip off. This motion creates a perfect peak to the frosting.

Once the frosting has been piped on top, chill the cupcakes for 15 to 30 minutes to set before adding your chosen decoration.

using a pastry bag and star tip

FROSTING CUPCAKES
USING A SMALL PALETTE KNIFE

Make sure the frosting is soft and spreadable.

Pile the equivalent of two palette-knives worth of frosting onto the top of the cupcake. Using a palette knife, spread the frosting over the top of the cupcake, scraping the palette knife straight down the edge of the paper cake case.

Using the palette knife, spread the frosting sideways around the top of the cupcake, slightly flattening the top but retaining the dome shape.

To finish, sweep the palette knife once around the sides of the cupcake along the ege of the paper cake case and then lift off.

Once the frosting has been spread on top, chill the cupcakes for 15 to 30 minutes to set before adding your chosen decoration.

ASSEMBLING LAYER CAKES

you will need

Cake leveler or large serrated knife
Nonslip turntable
Flat metal disk that is larger than the turntable
(I use the loose base of a springform cake pan)
Cake card the same size and shape as the cake
Pastry brush and pitcher (if the recipe requires sugar syrup)
Large flat palette knife
Metal side scraper

1 Evenly trim the tops of all the cake layers using either a cake leveler or large serrated knife.

2 Discard the trimmings. For light sponges, also trim the bottom off the middle layer to remove any dark crumb: this is not required for a dark chocolate cake. If any dark crumb is left on top of the cake after trimming, rub the surface in a circular motion using your hand held flat until the majority of the darker crumbs have come off.

3 Center a flat metal disk on top of a nonslip turntable, then place the cake card in the middle, securing it to the disk with a dab of buttercream or ganache. Spread a thin layer of buttercream or ganache over the cake card.

4 Lay the bottom cake layer on the cake card with the crumb side facing downward. If required by the recipe, brush the cake layer with sugar syrup.

5 Spoon the filling onto the middle of the cake layer. Using a large flat palette knife, spread the filling evenly outward from the middle by turning the turntable against the direction of the palette knife. Hold the palette knife edge parallel with the cake, but with the blade tilting upward slightly. Spread the filling evenly to a thickness of approximately ⅛ to ¼".

6 Lay the middle cake layer on top of the bottom layer; for a light sponge, this is the layer that has been trimmed on both top and bottom. If required by the recipe, brush the cake layer with sugar syrup.

7 Spread the filling over this middle cake layer, as in step 5, then lay the top cake layer on top of the middle layer with the crumb side facing upward. Press down gently with your hand held flat to remove any air pockets between the layers.

8 Spoon a generous amount of buttercream, frosting or ganache on top of the cake.

9 Using a large flat palette knife, spread the buttercream, frosting, or ganache over the surface of the cake as in step 5. Apply enough pressure to spread the coating thinly until the dark crumb shows through and the excess coating overlaps the edges.

10 Holding the palette knife vertically, push the overlapping coating down the sides of the cake. Spread the coating sideways using a back-and-forth paddling motion while turning the turntable against the direction of the palette knife.

11 Once the cake is covered, take a metal side scraper all around the sides in a single swoop to get them as straight as possible. Again, this should be a very thin layer that allows the dark crumb to show through.

12 Clean the top surface of the cake by scraping any excess coating from the edges toward the middle using the palette knife in a "flicking" motion. This first coat is called the crumb coat; its purpose is to hold any crumbs together and create a basic shape for the cake. The better the crumb coat, the better the final result. Chill the cake until the crumb coat has set, this may between 30 minutes and 1 hour.

13-14 For the final masking coat, cover the cake top and sides with clean, crumb-free buttercream, frosting, or ganache as in steps 9 and 10. Use enough coating so that no crumbs show through. You will need to work fast at this stage as the chilled crumb coat underneath will quickly set the masking coat.

15 Once the top and sides of the cake are masked, run a metal side scraper all round the sides in a single swoop as in step 11, holding the bottom edge of the side scraper against the cake card. If the results are not perfect the first time, repeat this step as it requires a little practice.

16 Clean the top surface of the cake as in step 12. Chill the cake in the refrigerator for 1 hour or until set.

ROYAL ICING

ingredients

Confectioners' sugar, sifted (see page 172)
Squeeze of lemon juice
Egg white or Meri-White powdered egg white (mixed with water as per the
directions on the package)

equipment

Electric mixer with paddle attachment
Rubber spatula
Medium-size bowl or plastic food storage container with lid
Clean damp cloth
Plastic wrap (optional)

Place the confectioners' sugar in the clean and grease-free bowl of an electric mixer together with the lemon juice and three-quarters of the egg white or Meri-White.

Mix on the lowest speed until combined. You may want to cover the mixing bowl with a cloth to prevent confectioners' sugar dust from going everywhere. If the mixture looks too dry, add a little more liquid until the icing looks smooth but not wet. After approximately 2 minutes, scrape the sides of the bowl to make sure the icing is well combined. Should the mixture still look too dry and grainy along the edges, add a little more liquid. Should the icing look slightly runny and glossy, adjust the consistency by adding a little sifted confectioners' sugar.

Continue mixing at the lowest speed for 4 to 5 minutes. Keep an eye on the consistency as royal icing can easily become overworked and overly aerated if mixed too long.

The royal icing is ready when stiff peaks appear around the sides of the bowl and you can hear a sloshing sound as the paddle moves the icing around. The icing should be smooth and satinlike in texture.

Transfer into a clean bowl or plastic food storage container and cover with a clean damp cloth. The icing can be stored for up to 1 week at room temperature if covered with a lid or plastic wrap.

....

FILLING A PASTRY BAG WITH ROYAL ICING

When filling a paper pastry bag with royal icing, use approximately 1 tablespoon at a time. The cleanest way to fill a bag is use a palette knife, scraping the icing down the folded edge of the pastry bag and letting it drop inside. With a clean palette knife, carefully push the icing down the bag as far as possible.

Once filled, flatten the open end of the pastry bag with the seam centered on one side.

Fold the top of the pastry bag over, away from the seam, and keep folding until you cannot fold any further to create tension on the bag; this tension will make it easier to pipe.

Store the filled pastry bag in a resealable plastic bag until ready to use. Once ready to pipe, snip a small section straight across the tip of the bag using a pair of sharp scissors.

....

tip

After being stored for a few days, the liquid and icing may separate. If this occurs, place the icing in the bowl of an electric mixer and mix on the lowest speed to bring it back together.

COLOR & CONSISTENCY

you will need

Royal icing
Small palette knife
Pitcher filled with water
Clean smooth work surface or flat disk for mixing, or use a small bowl
Paste or liquid food color
Plastic wrap or resealable plastic bag (optional)

COLORING ROYAL ICING

1 Place the royal icing onto a clean surface or flat disk next to a small amount of food color. Using a palette knife, pick up small amount of royal icing and mix it with the food color.

2 Work the food color through the icing, breaking down any tiny color specks as, if not mixed properly, these can burst and bleed as the icing dries.

3 Once mixed, add the colored icing a little at a time to the white icing and blend until you have achieved the required shade.

CONSISTENCY OF ROYAL ICING

4 To make soft-peak royal icing, dip the palette knife into water and mix it through until the icing looks a little glossy and forms peaks that fall over, yet still hold their shape. This consistency is for piping outlines, borders, and dots as well as for stenciling work.

5 To make runny royal icing, keep adding water until the icing looks shiny, flows together and flattens within 4 to 6 seconds. This consistency is perfect for flooding cookies.

MAKING A PAPER PASTRY BAG

Take a rectangular piece of silicone or waxed paper—approximately 12" by 18"—and cut it in half diagonally from one corner to the opposite corner. Rather than making a series of snips, slide the blades of the scissors through the paper to make a cleaner cut.

Hold one of the resulting paper triangles with your hand at the middle of the longest side and with your hand on the point on the opposite side. The longer side of the triangle should be on your left.

1 Curl the shorter corner on your right over to the corner that is pointing toward you, so that it forms a cone.

2 With your left hand, wrap the longer corner on the left around the tip of the cone twice.

3 Join the corner together with the other two corners at the back of the cone.

4 If the bag has an open tip at the point of the cone, close it by adjusting and tightening the inner and outer layers. Wiggle the layers back and forth until the cone forms a sharp point.

5 Fold the corners at the open end into the inside of the bag twice to prevent it unraveling.

tip

When filling, only ever half-fill the pastry bag otherwise the contents will ooze out when you squeeze. Once half-full, close the bag by folding the side with the seam over to the plain side twice.

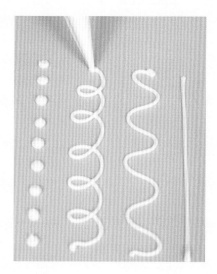

PIPING TECHNIQUES

The piping techniques demonstrated above are very useful to practice your general piping skills. Instead of piping directly onto a cookie or cake, simply take a piece of waxed paper and pipe onto that instead. You can also place templates underneath it and trace them through the paper with your pastry bag. If you have never piped with royal icing before, this task is a great way to train your skills, after all practice makes perfect.

First snip a small tip off your pastry bag already filled with icing. Hold the bag between the thumb and the fingers of your preferred hand; place your thumb over the folded end of the bag so that the bag stays firmly closed and place your index finger along the seam at the back of the bag. Use the index finger of your other hand to guide the tip.

PIPING LINES
Holding your bag at a 45-degree angle to the surface, touch the starting point with the tip of the bag and slowly squeeze out the icing. As you are squeezing, lift the bag up about 1in and guide the line straight toward you or, for

example, along the sides of a cookie. Once you are approaching the finishing point, gradually bring the bag down, stop squeezing and lay the line by touching the finishing point with the tip of the bag. This is called the lifting method.

PIPING DOTS
Hold the tip of your pastry bag $\frac{1}{32}''$ above the surface and squeeze out the icing to produce a dot on the surface. Keep the tip low inside the dot and allow the dot to spread to the required size. Once the dot has reached the required size, stop squeezing and lift off the tip while flicking it in a circular motion. Should the dot form a little peak at the top, flatten it carefully with a damp artist's brush.

PIPING LOOPS AND SWAGS
Start as you would for piping lines. Holding your bag almost vertically to the surface, touch the starting point with the tip and slowly squeeze out the icing. As you squeeze, lift the bag up by about 1″ and move it from one side to the other in circular movements, overlapping the lines in even intervals to create evenly spaced loops and swags.

tip

If you find it difficult to space the loops and swags out evenly, mark the points where the loops will meet and use them as guides.

THANK YOU

I have taken so much pride in writing this book, from the initial concept to creating the recipes and photographing at the Peggy Porschen Parlour, that I have cherished every single minute.

From the bottom of my heart, I would like to thank everyone who has helped to make **Boutique Baking** possible. As always, it has been a great team effort and I could not have done it without the help of some very special people.

I would like to thank my publisher and the team at Quadrille Publishing, Alison Cathie, Jane O'Shea, Helen Lewis, and Lisa Pendreigh for their shared enthusiasm and support in creating this book. As always, it's been wonderful working with you.

A big thank you to my favorite photographer, Georgia Glynn Smith, who has once again created magical pictures. To the very talented stylist Vicky Sullivan, for setting the perfect scene for my cakes. And to Helen Bratby for designing this beautiful book. I'm so glad you all have been part of the team as I could not have done it without you.

I also would like to thank the wonderful artist Carol Gillott for coming on board and providing such a beautiful illustration for the front cover. I have been a fan of her work for such a long time and I am thrilled to be working with her.

I would like to thank Mark Shipley for his invaluable guidance and business expertize. My colleague Stephanie Balls for assisting me with the initial concept for **Boutique Baking** and for always being at hand when I'm lost for words. A massive thank you goes to my talented baker Marianne Stewart, who has played a key role in developing some of the most delicious recipes in this book. And to my talented team of cake decorators, Cinthia Panariello, Franziska Thomczik, Maxie Giertz, Naomi Lee, and Nicola Fürle, who have all been invaluable throughout the entire production.

Thanks to my lovely retail angels, Zane Sniedze, Laura McGowan, Patience Harding, Reena Mathen, and Theresa Thomczik who all brightened up the pages with their beautiful smiles.

A big thank you goes to our model, the lovely Eleanor Jones for eating more Ice-Cream Cake Pops than any child at this age should and to Javier and Toni of By Appointment Only Design for contributing the most beautiful flower arrangements.

I would also like to take this as a special opportunity to thank the entire team at Peggy Porschen Cakes, it's been a fantastic first year and you have all helped in making the Parlour the best place to eat cake in London. Well that's what I think anyway. I feel blessed to have such a talented and enthusiastic team and I truly cherish working with all of you.

A very special thank you goes to my lovely great aunt Anita Leibel and her grandson Fabian, both have been tirelessly collecting the most beautiful vintage china pieces, many of which I have used as props in this book. Since, I have become so hooked on the whole vintage china thing and my collection is ever-growing.

I would like to thank my dad, Lee Pollock, Toni Franken, Brian Ma Siy, and Chalkley Calderwood for helping to turn my creative vision for the Parlour into reality and all of our suppliers who have supported us right from the start.

A heartfelt thank you to all of our customers, past and present, for your support and trust which has helped grow Peggy Porschen Cakes from a small business to the brand it is today.

Last but certainly not least, an overwhelming amount of gratitude goes to my family, for giving me all the strength and support I could ever wish for and more.

SUPPLIERS

Most of the equipment and ingredients used to create the cakes and confections in this book are available from specialist cake decorating suppliers and, increasingly, the more everyday items can be found in supermarkets and general cookware stores.

My own website—**www.peggyporschen.com**—includes an online store where you can purchase specialist cake decorating tools and ingredients, as well as an assortment of cookie cutters and other bakeware products. In addition, there is a small selection of handmade jams and exclusive loose-leaf tea blends available from Peggy's Pantry.

Throughout each year, I run a series of classes at the Peggy Porschen Academy. So whether you want to perfect your piping techniques to create irresistible cookies or brush up your baking skills to make heavenly cupcakes decorated with posies of spring flowers, there is a suitable course.

Peggy Porschen Academy
30 Elizabeth Street
Belgravia
London SW1W 9RB
www.peggyporschen.com

Each morning my team of specialist bakers freshly bake a range of layer cakes, cupcakes, cookies, and other yummy delights for visitors to the Peggy Porschen Parlour to either enjoy there and then with an artisan tea blend or coffee or to take away for a teatime treat. If you have enjoyed the recipes in this book, I hope you will pay us a visit.

Peggy Porschen Parlour
116 Ebury Street
Belgravia
London SW1W 9QQ
www.peggyporschen.com

INDEX